URIEL BRANDON

ESSENTIAL DOG BOARDING BUSINESS FOR BEGINNERS

A Practical Guide to Establishing and Growing a Successful Pet Care Service with Expert Tips on Sales Strategy, Operations, and Customer loyalty.

Copyright © 2024 by Uriel Brandon

All rights reserved. No part of this publication may be reproduced, stored or transmitted in any form or by any means, electronic, mechanical, photocopying, recording, scanning, or otherwise without written permission from the publisher. It is illegal to copy this book, post it to a website, or distribute it by any other means without permission.

First edition

This book was professionally typeset on Reedsy. Find out more at reedsy.com

Contents

Introduction	vii
1. Why Start a Dog Boarding Business?	vii
2. Overview of the Book: What You'll Learn	viii
CHAPTER 1: UNDERSTANDING THE DOG BOARDING INDUSTRY	1
1. What is Dog Boarding?	1
The Appeal of Dog Boarding	3
2. Market Trends and Opportunities	3
Key Market Trends	4
Opportunities in Dog Boarding	5
Challenge 1: High Competition	5
Solution: Differentiation Through Specialization and Quality	6
Challenge 2: Maintaining Dog Welfare	7
Solution: Prioritize Welfare Through Training, Safety, and Comfort	7
Challenge 3: Managing Operational Costs	9
Solution: Efficient Cost Management Without Sacrificing Quality	9
Challenge 4: Building Trust with Clients	11
Solution: Foster Trust Through Transparency, Communication, and Excellence	11
CHAPTER 2: CREATING A BUSINESS PLAN	13
Introduction to Business Planning	13
1. Defining Your Goals and Vision	14
Crafting Your Vision Statement	14

Setting Short-Term and Long-Term Goals	15
2. Budgeting and Financial Planning	16
Creating a Pricing Strategy	16
Financial Projections	18
3. Identifying Your Target Market	19
4. Competitive Analysis	20
Positioning Your Business	21
CHAPTER 3: SETTING UP YOUR DOG BOARDING FACILITY	23
1. Choosing the Right Location	24
Key Factors to Consider	24
Lease or Purchase?	25
2. Designing a Dog-Friendly Space	27
Essential Facility Areas	28
3. Necessary Permits and Licenses	28
Common Permits and Licenses	30
Steps to Obtain Permits	30
4. Equipment and Supplies	30
Essential Equipment	32
Additional Supplies	32
CHAPTER 4: LEGAL AND FINANCIAL CONSIDERATIONS	33
1. Registering Your Business	35
Steps to Register Your Business:	36
2. Understanding Zoning and Insurance Requirements	36
Pricing Your Services	38
Managing Taxes	40
CHAPTER 5: DEVELOPING SERVICES AND PACKAGES	43
CHAPTER 6: MARKETING AND BRANDING YOUR BUSINESS	51
Building an Online Presence	53
Local Advertising Tactics	55
Building Relationships with Veterinarians and Pet Stores	57
Key Takeaways	59
CHAPTER 7: DAY-TO-DAY OPERATIONS	61
Managing Bookings and Schedules	63

Feeding, Cleaning, and Exercising Dogs	65
Handling Emergencies	67
Ensuring Customer Satisfaction	69
Key Takeaways	71
CHAPTER 8: HIRING AND TRAINING STAFF	**72**
When to Hire Help	74
Training for Quality Pet Care	76
Creating a Positive Work Environment	78
Key Takeaways	81
CHAPTER 9: SCALING YOUR BUSINESS	**82**
Expanding Your Services	84
Adding New Locations	86
Building Long-Term Client Relationships	89
Key Takeaways	92
CHAPTER 10: REAL-LIFE TESTIMONIES FROM SUCCESSFUL DOG...	**93**
1. Inspiring Stories of Startups	95
Story 1: From Backyard Hobby to Thriving Business	95
Story 2: Turning Passion into a Franchise	96
Story 3: Innovating for Niche Clients	98
2. Lessons Learned from Mistakes and Successes	100
Lesson 1: The Importance of Planning	100
Lesson 2: Value Your Staff	102
Lesson 3: Listen to Customers	105
3. Advice for Beginners	107
Start with Passion but Build with Strategy	107
Don't Skimp on Quality	109
Stay Adaptable	109
Build a Network	111
Key Takeaways	112
CHAPTER 11: FAQS ABOUT STARTING A DOG BOARDING BUSINESS	**114**
1. Common Concerns from New Business Owners	114

   2. Answers to Legal, Financial, and Operational Questions   115
   3. Tips for Handling Difficult Situations   116
   Key Takeaways   117
CHAPTER 12: CREATING POLICIES AND CONTRACTS   118
   1. Establishing Clear Terms and Conditions   118
   2. Policies for Pet Health, Vaccinations, and Behavior   120
   3. Drafting Customer Agreements   122
   Best Practices for Policies and Contracts   124
   Key Takeaways   125
CHAPTER 13: MANAGING CUSTOMER RELATIONSHIPS   126
   1. Communication Tips with Pet Owners   128
   2. Handling Complaints and Feedback   130
   3. Building a Loyal Customer Base   133
   Key Takeaways   135
Chapter 14: The Importance of Reviews and Feedback   136
   1. Encouraging Positive Reviews   137
   2. Leveraging Testimonials to Attract New Clients   140
   3. Handling Negative Feedback Professionally   142
   Conclusion   144
Chapter 15: Emergency Preparedness and Crisis Management   145
   1. Dealing with Pet Illness or Injuries   147
   2. Preparing for Natural Disasters and Power Outages   149
   3. Communicating with Owners During Emergencies   152
   Conclusion   154
Conclusion   155

Introduction

Starting a dog boarding business is not just about caring for dogs—it's about tapping into a booming industry while pursuing a fulfilling, pet-focused career. With the rising demand for reliable pet care services, there's never been a better time to turn your love for animals into a thriving business. This book is your roadmap to building a successful dog boarding business from the ground up, whether you're a seasoned entrepreneur or someone new to the world of small business ownership.

1. Why Start a Dog Boarding Business?

The pet industry is experiencing unprecedented growth, fueled by pet owners who treat their furry companions as family. With more people traveling, working longer hours, or simply seeking high-quality care for their dogs, the need for trustworthy dog boarding facilities is skyrocketing.

The Rising Demand for Pet Care Services

Today, pets are considered part of the family, and their care is a top priority for owners. This shift has created a multi-billion-dollar pet care industry, where dog boarding plays a significant role. People want to leave their dogs in safe, comfortable, and well-managed environments, giving them peace of mind during their absence.

Benefits of Starting a Dog Boarding Business

Beyond the financial rewards, a dog boarding business offers several benefits:

- **Personal Fulfillment:** Enjoy the daily satisfaction of working with animals.
- **Flexibility:** Create your schedule and build a business that fits your lifestyle.
- **Community Impact:** Provide an essential service that brings value to your local community.
- **Growth Potential:** Expand your services to include grooming, training, or dog daycare as your business grows.

2. Overview of the Book: What You'll Learn

This book is designed to provide you with all the tools, knowledge, and strategies to start, run, and grow a successful dog boarding business. Each chapter dives deep into critical aspects of building your business, offering practical advice, actionable steps, and insider tips. Here's what you can expect to learn:

- **Business Basics:** Understand the essentials of starting a dog boarding business, including legal requirements, facility setup, and financial planning.
- **Operational Expertise:** Learn how to manage daily operations, care for dogs, and handle emergencies.
- **Marketing Strategies:** Discover effective ways to attract clients, build your brand, and grow your customer base.
- **Customer Retention:** Develop strategies for creating a loyal customer base through exceptional service.
- **Growth Opportunities:** Explore ways to expand your business and add new services for increased revenue.

Whether you're passionate about animals or looking for a lucrative business opportunity, this book is your comprehensive guide to making it happen. By the time you finish, you'll have the confidence and knowledge to turn your dog boarding business dreams into a successful reality.

CHAPTER 1: UNDERSTANDING THE DOG BOARDING INDUSTRY

Starting a dog boarding business starts with understanding the basics of the industry and what it takes to succeed. This chapter walks you through what dog boarding is all about, the current trends shaping the market, and the opportunities available to those who want to step into this field. It also highlights some of the challenges you might face along the way, helping you prepare for both the exciting and demanding aspects of running a business that caters to pets and their owners.

Whether you're passionate about working with dogs or drawn to the growing demand for pet care services, this chapter lays the groundwork to help you get started. By gaining a clear picture of the industry's landscape and understanding what it takes to provide a reliable, safe, and welcoming experience for your furry clients, you'll be ready to take the first steps toward building a successful business. This isn't just about caring for dogs—it's about building trust with pet owners and standing out in a competitive market.

1. What is Dog Boarding?

Dog boarding is all about providing a safe and comfortable place for dogs when their owners can't be with them. It's more than just offering a place for dogs to stay; it's about creating an environment where pets are treated with care and attention, so their owners feel reassured that their furry family members are in good hands. Many modern facilities go beyond the basics, offering cozy spaces, regular play sessions, and even personalized attention to make dogs feel right at home.

Running a dog boarding service means understanding the needs of both the pets and their owners. Dogs thrive on routine, affection, and stimulation, and a good facility makes sure they get all three. Whether it's providing a quiet space for older dogs or active playtime for energetic pups, the goal is to keep the dogs happy and healthy while they're away from their families. For owners, it's about trust—knowing their pets are being cared for as if they were your own.

A big part of the job involves creating an environment where dogs can relax and enjoy themselves. This means everything from having clean and comfortable sleeping areas to maintaining a safe space for them to play and socialize with other dogs. It's also about understanding each dog's personality—some might be shy or nervous, while others are outgoing and ready to make friends. Tailoring the care to fit these individual needs makes a huge difference in the overall experience.

Beyond the care you provide to the dogs, there's also the human side of dog boarding. Pet owners want to feel connected and informed while their dogs are with you. Regular updates, photos, and open communication go a long way in building trust and ensuring owners feel confident about their decision to leave their pets in your care. It's not just about running a business; it's about building relationships with the people who trust you with their beloved pets.

In the end, dog boarding is about striking the right balance—offering a professional, well-run service while making everything feel personal and thoughtful. When you put care and attention into every detail, from the facilities to the way you interact with dogs and their owners, you create an experience that keeps customers coming back and helps your business thrive. It's a responsibility and a rewarding opportunity to make a positive difference in the lives of both pets and their people.

The Appeal of Dog Boarding

- Convenience: Pet owners can travel or attend to responsibilities without worrying about their dogs.
    - Peace of Mind: Knowing their pets are in capable hands.
    - Personalized Care: Many facilities provide tailored services to suit individual dog needs.

2. Market Trends and Opportunities

The pet care industry, especially dog boarding, has been expanding rapidly as more people view their pets as family members. With pet ownership on the rise, particularly among younger generations, the demand for quality pet care services continues to grow. Many dog owners are looking for boarding options that go beyond the traditional kennel experience, prioritizing comfort, safety, and individualized care for their furry companions. This shift in expectations has created space for businesses to innovate and offer premium services that cater to these needs.

One of the driving factors behind this growth is the increase in disposable income, allowing pet owners to spend more on their pets' wellbeing. People are willing to pay extra for facilities that offer a home-like environment, socialization opportunities, and add-ons like grooming or training sessions. Additionally, the growing trend of pet-friendly travel means owners are seeking reliable boarding options when they can't take their dogs along. As a result, businesses that provide flexible, high-quality care are seeing more opportunities to thrive.

Another significant trend is the use of technology in the pet care industry. From online booking platforms to apps that allow owners to check in on their dogs via webcams, technology has become an essential part of the boarding experience. Offering these conveniences not only appeals to tech-savvy customers but also builds trust by keeping owners connected with their pets. Staying updated on these tools and incorporating them into your business can give you a competitive edge.

The rise of specialized services also presents opportunities for dog boarding businesses to stand out. For instance, some facilities cater specifically to small breeds, senior dogs, or those with special needs. Others emphasize eco-friendly practices, such as sustainable materials and organic food options. By identifying a niche within the market, you can tailor your services to meet specific customer demands and create a loyal client base.

Understanding these trends is essential for positioning your business in the best possible way. By staying in tune with what customers are looking for and being open to innovation, you can capitalize on the growing demand for quality dog boarding services. This isn't just about meeting expectations—it's about exceeding them and creating an experience that keeps both pets and their owners happy.

Key Market Trends

- Humanization of Pets: Pet owners increasingly treat their pets as family, seeking high-quality care.
    - Increased Travel: With more people traveling for work or leisure, the demand for boarding services is rising.
    - Technology Integration: Apps and platforms allow customers to book services, receive updates, and review facilities conveniently.

- Sustainable Practices: Eco-friendly services, like sustainable pet bedding and waste management, appeal to environmentally-conscious pet owners.

Opportunities in Dog Boarding

- Specialized Services: Catering to senior dogs, puppies, or pets with special needs.
  - Additional Offerings: Grooming, training, and daycare to diversify revenue streams.
  - Mobile Boarding: Bringing services directly to the customer's home for convenience.

3. Key Challenges and How to Overcome Them
   Running a dog boarding business can be rewarding, but it's not without challenges. Recognizing potential hurdles early on and developing strategies to address them is critical for long-term success.

Challenge 1: High Competition

With the booming demand for pet care, competition in the industry has become more intense than ever. Big players dominate the market with extensive resources, while smaller, niche providers are emerging with unique offerings. This saturated environment makes it difficult for new businesses to gain traction and for existing ones to maintain customer loyalty.

Solution: Differentiation Through Specialization and Quality

To overcome high competition, businesses need to adopt a strategic approach:

1. Identify a Niche Market:
   - Focus on underserved areas in the pet care industry. For example, specialize in senior pet care, exotic pet services, organic pet food, or eco-friendly grooming products. Catering to a specific need helps your business stand out and builds loyalty among a targeted customer base.

2. Exceptional Customer Service:
   - Personalized experiences go a long way in creating loyal customers. Offer services such as one-on-one consultations, follow-ups after visits, or special perks like birthday treats for pets. Building strong relationships with clients through empathy and attentiveness ensures they choose your business over competitors.

3. Unique Offerings:
   - Stand out by introducing services or products that competitors don't offer. For instance, pet fitness tracking, subscription-based care packages, or holistic treatments like pet massage or acupuncture can set you apart. Being innovative helps attract and retain customers who value exclusivity.

4. Leverage Technology:
   - Create user-friendly apps or platforms that simplify pet care, like scheduling appointments, tracking pet health, or delivering pet supplies. Tech-savvy features enhance convenience and can make your business the go-to choice for busy pet owners.

5. Emphasize Your Brand Story:
   - In a crowded market, customers connect with businesses that have authentic stories. Highlight your passion for animals, your journey in the

pet care industry, or your mission to improve pet welfare. A strong brand identity fosters trust and loyalty.

By tailoring your approach and offering something truly special, you can turn the challenge of high competition into an opportunity to carve out a unique position in the pet care market.

Challenge 2: Maintaining Dog Welfare

The health, safety, and overall well-being of the dogs in your care are central to building trust with pet owners and establishing a positive reputation. However, achieving this consistently requires dedication, expertise, and attention to detail.

Solution: Prioritize Welfare Through Training, Safety, and Comfort

1. Invest in Proper Training:
   - All staff should be thoroughly trained in dog behavior, first aid, and care practices. This ensures they can handle various situations, from managing anxious dogs to responding to medical emergencies.
   - Regular workshops and certifications, such as canine CPR or animal behavior courses, help staff stay updated on best practices.
   - Educate staff to recognize signs of distress or illness early, allowing prompt intervention and prevention of serious issues.

2. Adhere to Strict Safety Protocols:
   - Implement clear procedures for handling dogs during play, feeding, and transportation to minimize risks of injury or stress.

- Use secure enclosures and equipment to prevent escapes or accidents.
- Establish emergency plans, including accessible veterinary support, evacuation protocols, and backup systems for power outages or extreme weather.

3. Maintain Clean and Comfortable Facilities:
   - Regularly clean and disinfect all areas to prevent the spread of diseases, pests, or unpleasant odors.
   - Provide cozy, temperature-controlled spaces with adequate ventilation for resting and sleeping.
   - Use non-toxic, pet-safe cleaning products to ensure the environment remains healthy.

4. Prioritize Enrichment and Socialization:
   - Design activities that stimulate dogs both physically and mentally, such as obstacle courses, group play sessions, or individual cuddle times.
   - Carefully match dogs by size, temperament, and play style during group activities to ensure positive interactions and avoid conflicts.

5. Communicate with Pet Owners:
   - Share daily updates with owners through photos, videos, or reports to reassure them of their dog's well-being.
   - Provide tailored advice on maintaining dog welfare at home, strengthening your role as a trusted partner in their pet's care.

By focusing on these key areas, you create an environment where dogs feel safe, healthy, and happy, which not only enhances their well-being but also builds lasting trust with their owners.

CHAPTER 1: UNDERSTANDING THE DOG BOARDING INDUSTRY

Challenge 3: Managing Operational Costs

Running a boarding facility comes with substantial financial demands, from paying staff salaries and utility bills to maintaining the facility and purchasing supplies. These costs can quickly add up, threatening profitability if not managed effectively.

Solution: Efficient Cost Management Without Sacrificing Quality

1. Adopt a Scalable Business Model:
   - Start small and expand as demand grows. Begin with a limited number of boarding spaces and gradually invest in additional amenities or services as your customer base increases.
   - Offer tiered pricing plans, such as basic boarding versus premium packages with added perks, to cater to diverse budgets while maximizing revenue potential.

2. Conduct Regular Expense Reviews:
   - Periodically audit your operational costs to identify areas where savings can be made. For instance, evaluate utility usage, subscription services, or supply vendors.
   - Negotiate with suppliers for bulk discounts or better rates, especially for recurring expenses like food, cleaning supplies, and bedding.

3. Embrace Cost-Effective Solutions:
   - Invest in energy-efficient appliances and lighting to reduce utility bills.
   - Implement water-saving systems for cleaning and pet bathing to lower water usage.
   - Utilize durable, long-lasting materials for furniture and equipment to

minimize replacement costs over time.

4. Streamline Staff Management:
   - Cross-train staff to handle multiple roles, such as caregiving, cleaning, and administrative tasks, ensuring efficient use of labor.
   - Schedule staff based on peak and non-peak hours to optimize coverage while avoiding overstaffing during quieter times.

5. Explore Supplemental Income Streams:
   - Offer additional services like grooming, training, or retail products (e.g., toys, food, or treats) to diversify revenue sources.
   - Partner with local pet businesses or veterinarians for referral programs or co-branded services.

6. Leverage Technology for Efficiency:
   - Use software to manage bookings, payments, and client communication, reducing administrative burdens and associated costs.
   - Automate repetitive tasks, such as feeding schedules or inventory tracking, to save time and labor.

7. Monitor Maintenance Proactively:
   - Conduct regular facility inspections to catch and address minor issues before they escalate into costly repairs.
   - Establish a routine maintenance plan for equipment like HVAC systems, grooming tools, and enclosures.

By employing these strategies, you can effectively manage operational costs while maintaining high-quality services. This balance ensures long-term sustainability and profitability for your boarding facility.

CHAPTER 1: UNDERSTANDING THE DOG BOARDING INDUSTRY

Challenge 4: Building Trust with Clients

For pet owners, their animals are family members, making it essential for them to feel confident and secure when leaving their pets in someone else's care. Establishing and maintaining trust is a crucial challenge, especially for new or growing businesses in the pet care industry.

Solution: Foster Trust Through Transparency, Communication, and Excellence

1. Be Transparent About Your Services and Facility:
   - Offer tours of your facility so pet owners can see where their pets will stay. Highlight cleanliness, safety measures, and amenities during these tours.
   - Clearly outline policies, pricing, and what's included in your services to avoid misunderstandings. For example, explain feeding routines, play schedules, and emergency protocols upfront.
   - Provide credentials, such as staff certifications in animal care or partnerships with veterinarians, to demonstrate professionalism and expertise.

2. Maintain Open and Regular Communication:
   - Keep clients updated with daily reports, photos, or videos of their pets enjoying activities, eating, or relaxing. This reassurance helps build trust and alleviates their anxiety.
   - Use technology like apps or messaging platforms to make it easy for clients to check in, ask questions, or receive updates.
   - Proactively inform clients about any incidents, no matter how minor, and explain how they were handled to demonstrate accountability.

3. Build a Proven Track Record:
   - Encourage satisfied clients to leave reviews or testimonials online.

Positive feedback from other pet owners goes a long way in building credibility.
- Highlight success stories, such as helping a nervous dog adjust to boarding or accommodating special medical needs, to showcase your expertise and compassion.
- Create a referral program to reward existing clients for recommending your services, showing your confidence in your care.

4. Provide Personalized Experiences:
- Show clients that you understand their pets' unique needs by tailoring services to their preferences, such as offering specific diets, play routines, or quiet spaces for anxious animals.
- Remember small details, like the pet's birthday or favorite toy, to demonstrate genuine care and attention.

5. Offer Consistency and Reliability:
- Ensure your services and staff maintain high standards of care every time. Consistency reassures clients that their pets will always receive the best treatment.
- Stick to promised schedules and agreements, such as drop-off and pick-up times, to show respect for clients' time and trust.

By prioritizing transparency, communication, and a client-focused approach, you can establish strong relationships with pet owners. This not only builds trust but also creates loyal customers who are likely to recommend your services to others.

By understanding the fundamentals of the dog boarding industry, its trends, and how to overcome challenges, you'll be well-prepared to navigate the competitive landscape and lay the groundwork for a successful business.

CHAPTER 2: CREATING A BUSINESS PLAN

Introduction to Business Planning

Starting a dog boarding business is more than just a passion for pets—it requires a clear and actionable plan to succeed. I've learned that a solid business plan isn't just a formality; it's the foundation for every decision you'll make along the way. It's your roadmap, guiding you through the challenges and opportunities of starting, running, and growing your venture.

In this chapter, I'll walk you through how I approach defining goals and crafting a vision, setting realistic budgets, identifying the perfect target market, and analyzing the competition. These steps aren't just theoretical; they're practical strategies that have worked for me and can work for you. Whether you're just getting started or looking to refine your existing operations, I'll share insights that will help you build a thriving dog boarding business with confidence.

1. Defining Your Goals and Vision

Every successful business starts with a clear vision and set of goals. These elements define your business's purpose and guide your decisions.

Crafting Your Vision Statement

Crafting a vision statement for your dog boarding business is an important step in shaping its future and guiding its direction. Your vision statement serves as a clear expression of your long-term goals and the values that drive your business. It reflects not only what you aim to provide for your customers but also the kind of atmosphere you want to create for their pets. A well-crafted vision helps you stay focused and motivated, as it becomes a roadmap for success. It's important that this statement speaks to your core values, providing a sense of purpose for both your team and your customers.

When thinking about your vision statement, consider the key elements that are most important for a dog boarding service. Safety and comfort should be top priorities. You want owners to feel confident that their pets will be in a secure environment, whether they are staying for a few hours or a few days. This can include things like secure fencing, well-maintained facilities, and staff who are trained in handling and caring for dogs of various temperaments and sizes. It's also essential to create a space where dogs can enjoy themselves, whether that's through playtime, rest, or socializing with other dogs.

Another critical factor is establishing trust with the pet owners. A great vision statement reassures them that their pets will not only be safe but also well cared for. Owners want to know that their dogs will be comfortable and that their needs will be met in their absence. Clear communication is key here, and you can make it a part of your vision to provide regular updates or photos to keep owners at ease. This kind of transparency builds a solid relationship with your clients and can lead to repeat business and positive word-of-mouth.

At the same time, the atmosphere of your business should be one that reflects warmth and friendliness. Whether it's in your physical space or the way your team interacts with clients, the goal is to create an environment where both pets and their owners feel welcomed and appreciated. The right tone can make all the difference when it comes to customer loyalty. If owners feel that their pets are treated like family, they're more likely to return and recommend your services to others. Your vision statement should reflect this commitment to a welcoming and friendly environment.

Finally, as your dog boarding business grows, your vision statement can help guide decisions about expanding services or improving existing offerings. It serves as a reminder of why you started the business in the first place and keeps everyone aligned with your goals. Over time, you may adjust your vision as you learn from experience and better understand the needs of your customers. Ultimately, the vision statement should inspire both your team and your clients, helping everyone involved feel confident that they are part of something meaningful and beneficial.

Setting Short-Term and Long-Term Goals

- Short-Term Goals: These may include securing a location, obtaining necessary permits, and attracting your first customers.
    - Long-Term Goals: Expanding services, opening additional locations, or becoming the go-to boarding facility in your area.

A well-defined vision and clear goals not only keep you focused but also inspire confidence in potential investors and customers.

2. Budgeting and Financial Planning

Proper financial planning is essential to ensure your business remains sustainable. Start by estimating your initial startup costs and ongoing expenses.

Startup Costs
 - Facility rental or purchase
 - Renovations and equipment (kennels, bedding, toys, cleaning supplies)
 - Licensing and permits
 - Marketing and branding materials

Ongoing Expenses
 - Utilities and maintenance
 - Employee salaries
 - Insurance
 - Supplies and amenities for the dogs

Creating a Pricing Strategy

Creating a pricing strategy for your dog boarding business requires a balanced approach that takes both your costs and the local market into account. Start by rescarching what other businesses in your area are charging for similar services. This gives you a good idea of what customers are willing to pay and ensures you stay competitive. Keep in mind that setting your prices too high might turn potential customers away, while prices that are too low could undervalue your services or lead to financial challenges. Understanding the local market will help you find that sweet spot where your pricing is both fair and profitable.

Once you have a sense of the local market, it's important to consider your own business costs. These include rent or mortgage for your facility, staff wages, utilities, insurance, and the care products you provide to dogs, such as food, toys, or bedding. You need to set a price that not only covers these expenses but also allows for a reasonable profit margin. Factor in any additional overheads and make sure to regularly review your pricing to keep it aligned with any changes in your costs. The goal is to find a price point that allows your business to run smoothly while still remaining accessible to your customers.

Offering tiered pricing based on services or amenities is another great way to structure your pricing. For instance, you could offer a basic rate for standard boarding services, such as a comfortable kennel or room, and then offer premium options for extra services like grooming, one-on-one playtime, or additional space for larger dogs. This allows customers to choose the level of service that fits their needs and budget. Tiered pricing can also appeal to a wider range of customers, from those looking for basic care to those willing to pay extra for luxury options.

It's also a good idea to provide discounts for longer stays or repeat customers. For example, offering a reduced rate for customers who book for a week or more can help incentivize long-term bookings. Loyalty programs or referral discounts can also encourage customers to return or recommend your services to others. These types of incentives can help build a strong customer base and encourage repeat business, which is crucial for the growth and stability of your dog boarding service.

Lastly, don't forget to continuously evaluate and adjust your pricing strategy as your business grows. As your reputation builds and you gain more experience, you may find that you can raise your prices without losing customers. Alternatively, you might discover that certain services or packages are more popular than others, allowing you to adjust your offerings. Keeping an eye on your competitors and staying open to customer feedback can help you refine your pricing strategy over time, ensuring that you remain competitive while still meeting the needs of your business.

Financial Projections

Creating financial projections for your dog boarding business is a crucial step in planning for success. By outlining realistic revenue and expense projections, you'll be able to assess your potential profitability and make informed decisions for the future. Start by estimating how many dogs you can board on a daily, weekly, or monthly basis, based on the size of your facility and staffing capabilities. Multiply that by your expected rates to calculate your potential revenue. For example, if you charge $30 per day and can board 10 dogs each day, your daily revenue would be $300. Multiply that by the number of days you expect to operate each month to get a clearer picture of your monthly and annual revenue.

On the expense side, it's important to account for all costs associated with running your dog boarding business. This includes fixed expenses such as rent or mortgage, utilities, insurance, and staff wages. Additionally, you'll need to factor in variable expenses like food, cleaning supplies, maintenance costs, and any marketing or advertising efforts. Setting aside a portion of your income for unexpected costs, such as repairs or seasonal fluctuations in business, is also a good idea. Calculating these expenses accurately will help you determine how much of your revenue will go toward covering your costs, and how much can contribute to your profit margin.

When projecting your revenue and expenses, it's essential to be realistic and conservative. Avoid overestimating the number of dogs you'll be able to board or underestimating the costs associated with running the business. New businesses, in particular, can face periods of lower-than-expected income, especially in the early months. Consider seasonal variations in demand as well. For example, you might see higher demand during holidays or school breaks, and slower periods during the off-season. By factoring in these fluctuations, you can plan more effectively for months when income may be lower.

Once you've created an initial set of revenue and expense projections, take time to analyze them for areas where you can improve efficiency or save costs. For example, you might notice that your staffing costs are higher than expected, which could indicate the need to adjust your staffing levels or improve scheduling. Alternatively, you may identify an area where you can invest in a service or amenity that can bring in more revenue, such as offering grooming services or expanding your facility to accommodate more dogs. Regularly reviewing and adjusting your financial projections will help you stay on track and ensure your business remains profitable.

Finally, these financial projections are not only useful for your internal planning, but they can also be valuable when seeking funding or investment. If you're looking to secure a loan or attract investors, presenting detailed and realistic financial projections demonstrates that you have a clear understanding of your business's potential and the challenges you might face. It shows that you're prepared to make smart decisions based on data and have a roadmap in place to achieve your financial goals. Having these projections in place will help you navigate your first year more confidently and set a solid foundation for the growth of your dog boarding business.

3. Identifying Your Target Market

Understanding your target audience is key to attracting the right customers and meeting their needs.

Demographics
  - Pet owners aged 25–55
  - Middle- to upper-income households

- Professionals, frequent travelers, or families with busy schedules

Psychographics
- Pet owners who treat their dogs like family
- Individuals seeking high-quality, reliable care for their pets

Customer Needs
- Safe and comfortable boarding environments
- Personalized care and attention
- Transparency and communication during their pet's stay

By identifying your target market, you can tailor your services and marketing efforts to attract the ideal clientele.

4. Competitive Analysis

To succeed in the dog boarding industry, you need to understand your competition and find ways to differentiate your business.

Researching Competitors
- Visit local boarding facilities to observe their operations and offerings.
- Analyze their pricing, services, and customer reviews.
- Identify their strengths and weaknesses.

Finding Your Unique Selling Proposition (USP)
Your USP is what sets your business apart. It could be:
- Offering specialized care for senior dogs or puppies.
- Providing luxury boarding options with premium amenities.
- Emphasizing eco-friendly practices.

CHAPTER 2: CREATING A BUSINESS PLAN

Positioning Your Business

Positioning your dog boarding business effectively in the market is essential to stand out from competitors and attract customers. The key to successful positioning is identifying gaps in the current market and finding ways to meet customer needs better than your competitors. Start by doing a thorough analysis of other dog boarding services in your area. Look at their offerings, prices, customer reviews, and the overall experience they provide. Are there any aspects they may be lacking in or areas where you think you could improve? This type of competitive analysis can reveal opportunities to position your business in a way that appeals to potential customers who are dissatisfied with existing options.

For instance, if you find that most local facilities don't offer ample outdoor play areas or sufficient space for dogs to run and exercise, this could be a significant selling point for your business. Investing in a large, safe, and well-maintained outdoor play area where dogs can enjoy regular exercise and socialize with other pets might make your boarding service more appealing. Pet owners are often looking for a place where their dogs can not only be safely cared for but also have fun and get plenty of exercise. By positioning your business as one that prioritizes these needs, you can attract customers who are willing to pay more for these added benefits.

Another way to differentiate your business is by offering superior customer service. If your competitors have long response times or lack personalized communication, you could position your business as one that offers exceptional customer care. This might include providing regular updates on the dog's well-being, sending photos or videos, or offering a direct line of communication for owners to check in at any time. Customer experience plays a huge role in building trust and loyalty, and positioning yourself as a business that goes the extra mile in communication can help set you apart from others in the area.

Additionally, consider offering value-added services that your competitors may not provide. This could include special amenities like premium bedding, grooming services, or individualized care for dogs with special needs, such as older dogs or those with anxiety. These services not only help to enhance the pet's experience but also increase your revenue streams. By offering something extra that's hard to find elsewhere, you make your facility more attractive to customers who want to ensure their pets receive the highest level of care.

Finally, it's important to continually monitor the market and adjust your positioning as needed. Trends in the pet care industry evolve, and customer preferences can shift over time. Stay connected with your customers, ask for feedback, and pay attention to the evolving needs of pet owners. This allows you to adjust your offerings and services to stay ahead of the competition and continually provide better value. By regularly reassessing your position in the market and staying adaptable, you can ensure your dog boarding business remains competitive and continues to attract loyal customers.

By creating a detailed business plan with clear goals, sound financial planning, a well-defined target market, and a competitive strategy, you'll set the stage for a thriving dog boarding business.

CHAPTER 3: SETTING UP YOUR DOG BOARDING FACILITY

When I first started my dog boarding business, I quickly realized that creating a safe, welcoming, and efficient facility was the foundation of my success. Every decision I made—from choosing the location to setting up the space—played a vital role in ensuring not only the comfort and safety of the dogs but also the trust and satisfaction of their owners.

In this chapter, I'll walk you through the critical steps I took to build my facility from the ground up. I'll share how I chose the perfect location, keeping both convenience and safety in mind. I'll talk about the process of designing a space that wasn't just functional but also inviting and dog-friendly. I'll explain how I navigated the sometimes-overwhelming world of permits and licenses, ensuring my business was compliant and professional from day one. Finally, I'll cover the equipment and supplies that I found essential for running a smooth operation.

By the end of this chapter, you'll have a clear roadmap for creating a facility that dogs love, owners trust, and you can be proud of. Let's dive in!

—-

1. Choosing the Right Location

When I set out to establish my dog boarding facility, one of the biggest decisions I faced was choosing the right location. It wasn't just about finding a spot on a map—it was about understanding the needs of my future clients and their dogs. I had to think about convenience, not just for me, but for the pet owners who would be dropping off and picking up their furry companions. A place that was easy to access, yet far enough from busy traffic, made all the difference.

I also considered the surrounding environment. Dogs thrive in spaces where they feel safe and calm, so I looked for an area that wasn't too noisy or crowded. The last thing I wanted was for anxious barking to echo through a densely packed neighborhood. At the same time, I thought about visibility. A well-placed facility could draw attention and build trust simply by being in the right spot.

Finding the perfect location wasn't just about external factors, though. I needed to ensure there was enough room to bring my vision to life. A spacious lot meant I could create play areas, comfortable kennels, and designated zones for different activities. Balancing all these factors was a challenge, but it was worth every bit of effort. The location I chose became more than just a place—it became a welcoming home away from home for every dog that walked through the door.

Key Factors to Consider

- Accessibility: Choose a location that's easy for customers to find and reach. Proximity to residential areas, highways, or popular dog parks can be a significant advantage.
    - Space Requirements: Ensure the property has ample space for boarding,

play areas, and potential expansion.
  - Zoning Regulations: Verify that the property complies with local zoning laws for pet-related businesses.
  - Safety and Security: Select a site in a safe neighborhood with features like secure fencing and proper lighting.

Lease or Purchase?

When deciding whether to lease or purchase the property for your dog boarding business, there are several factors to consider, such as your budget, long-term goals, and the level of stability or flexibility you desire. Both leasing and purchasing have their advantages and drawbacks, so it's important to align your decision with the specific needs of your business and the direction you envision for the future.

Leasing a property can offer greater flexibility, especially in the early stages of your business. With a lease, you avoid the large upfront costs associated with purchasing real estate, which can be a significant barrier for new businesses. Leasing allows you to invest your capital in other areas, such as marketing, equipment, or staffing, rather than tying up funds in property. Additionally, leases often come with shorter terms, allowing you to reassess your location after a few years to see if the space still fits your needs or if you want to expand. This flexibility is particularly beneficial if your business is still in the early stages or if you expect changes in demand over time. Leasing can also provide some protection against the unpredictable nature of real estate markets, as property values or rents might fluctuate.

On the other hand, purchasing the property gives you stability and potential long-term financial benefits. If you plan on growing your dog boarding business over time and want to secure your operating location, buying a property can provide a sense of permanence. As a property owner, you won't have to worry about rent increases or lease renewals, which can be a concern when leasing in areas with rising demand or limited space. Owning your property also means you have control over any modifications or improvements you may want to make to better suit your business needs. Over time, real estate can appreciate, meaning that purchasing a property can also serve as an investment that could potentially offer returns if the property's value increases.

When deciding whether to lease or buy, it's also important to assess your budget and cash flow. Purchasing a property typically requires a significant upfront investment, including a down payment, closing costs, and possibly renovation expenses. Additionally, mortgage payments and property taxes are ongoing costs to consider. If your business is in its infancy or you don't have the financial resources to manage these costs, leasing might be a safer option, as it generally involves less financial risk. On the other hand, if you have the capital and your business is stable or growing, buying could be a smart move, as it allows you to build equity over time.

Another factor to consider is the location of the property. If you lease a property, you might have more flexibility to move if the location turns out to be less than ideal or if demand shifts in your area. However, purchasing a property locks you into a specific location for the long term, which could be either an advantage or a disadvantage depending on how well the location works for your business. If you choose to buy, you'll need to be confident that the location is not only suitable for your current needs but will also continue to attract customers as your business grows.

Ultimately, whether you lease or purchase the property comes down to your long-term vision and your financial situation. Leasing offers flexibility and fewer financial commitments, making it ideal for new or smaller businesses, while purchasing offers long-term stability and the potential for investment growth. Carefully consider your business's needs, future plans, and financial capacity before making this important decision. If you're unsure, it might be worth consulting with a financial advisor or real estate expert to help weigh the pros and cons specific to your situation.

—-

2. Designing a Dog-Friendly Space

When I began designing my dog boarding facility, I knew it wasn't just about making it look good—it had to feel right for the dogs and function seamlessly for day-to-day operations. I imagined the space from a dog's perspective, considering what would make them feel safe, comfortable, and happy while staying with me. Every detail, from the layout to the materials I used, was chosen with their well-being in mind.

Safety came first. I made sure that every area was secure, with sturdy fencing and gates to prevent any unexpected escapes. The flooring had to be durable, easy to clean, and gentle on paws, so I carefully avoided materials that could become slippery or too rough. Ventilation was another priority. I knew that good air circulation wasn't just about keeping odors at bay—it was about ensuring the health and comfort of every dog in my care.

At the same time, I thought about how the space could work efficiently for me and my staff. Clear pathways, strategically placed storage, and designated areas for feeding, play, and rest made everything flow smoothly. I wanted a facility where dogs could enjoy themselves without feeling overcrowded, so I planned for plenty of room to roam and interact.

What I loved most about the process was creating spaces where each dog could feel at ease. Cozy resting areas with soft bedding, shaded outdoor spots for warm days, and playful zones where energy could run wild—all these elements came together to make the facility more than just a boarding space. It became a place where dogs could thrive.

Essential Facility Areas

- Reception Area: Create a welcoming space for clients to drop off and pick up their pets. Include a seating area and a front desk.
  - Boarding Kennels: Design individual kennels or suites that provide comfort, ventilation, and privacy. Ensure easy cleaning and maintenance.
  - Outdoor Play Areas: Provide secure, fenced spaces where dogs can exercise and socialize.
  - Feeding and Rest Zones: Allocate quiet areas for feeding and resting, away from high-traffic spaces.
  - Staff Areas: Include break rooms, storage areas, and administrative offices for employees.

Design Tips for Dog Comfort and Safety
  - Use non-slip flooring and durable, pet-safe materials.
  - Install soundproofing to minimize noise and stress.
  - Incorporate natural lighting and ventilation where possible.

—-

3. Necessary Permits and Licenses

Running a dog boarding business involves following various rules and regulations to ensure everything is done legally and responsibly. The specific permits and licenses required can vary depending on your location, but they typically include a general business license, a kennel license, and zoning approval. These documents confirm that your business meets the legal standards for safety, sanitation, and animal care, which is crucial for building trust with your clients. It's important to research your local government's requirements and ensure all paperwork is in place before opening your doors.

CHAPTER 3: SETTING UP YOUR DOG BOARDING FACILITY

In many cases, zoning laws determine whether your property is suitable for a dog boarding facility. You may need to provide proof that the location will not cause noise disturbances or other issues in the neighborhood. Some areas might also require inspections to ensure your premises meet specific health and safety standards. These inspections are designed to check for secure fencing, adequate space, and proper ventilation, among other things. Taking these steps not only keeps you compliant but also creates a safer environment for the dogs in your care.

Beyond local permits, you might need additional licenses depending on the services you offer. For instance, if you provide grooming or training, separate certifications or permits could be required. Similarly, if you plan to sell pet supplies or food, there may be retail-specific regulations to follow. It's a good idea to consult with a business attorney or local officials to ensure you've covered every base. Being thorough in this process can save you from future headaches, such as fines or interruptions to your business operations.

Another important consideration is liability insurance, which may be a legal requirement in some areas. Even if it's not mandatory, it's a wise investment to protect yourself against unexpected situations. Dogs can be unpredictable, and having insurance can provide peace of mind if an accident or injury occurs. It's also worth exploring bonding options to demonstrate to clients that you take their trust seriously. These added measures can make your business stand out and attract more customers.

Taking care of the legal and regulatory aspects might feel overwhelming, but it's a critical step in building a successful dog boarding business. Proper licensing and permits not only show that you're serious about your work but also ensure you're operating ethically. By investing time and effort into understanding and meeting these requirements, you're setting a solid foundation for a business that can grow with confidence and credibility.

Common Permits and Licenses

- Business License: Obtain a general business license to operate legally.
  - Animal Care Permit: Some areas require specific permits for boarding or caring for animals.
  - Zoning Permit: Ensure your facility complies with local zoning requirements.
  - Health and Safety Inspections: Schedule inspections to certify that your facility meets sanitation and safety standards.

Steps to Obtain Permits

- Research local regulations and requirements.
  - Submit applications with the necessary documentation.
  - Pay any applicable fees and undergo inspections.

Staying compliant helps you avoid legal issues and builds trust with customers.

—-

4. Equipment and Supplies

Setting up a dog boarding business requires careful planning when it comes to choosing the right equipment and supplies. These items play a significant role in creating a safe, clean, and comfortable environment for the dogs. Basic necessities include sturdy kennels or crates, comfortable bedding, and plenty of food and water bowls. The quality of these items matters because they contribute to the well-being of the dogs in your care. Durable and easy-to-clean materials are a smart choice to ensure long-term use and maintain

CHAPTER 3: SETTING UP YOUR DOG BOARDING FACILITY

hygiene standards.

Beyond the basics, consider items that enhance the dogs' overall experience. This includes toys for mental stimulation, grooming tools for daily upkeep, and waste disposal systems to keep the area clean. Exercise is crucial for a dog's health, so having a designated play area with secure fencing is essential. Depending on the size of your facility, you might also invest in agility equipment or interactive play structures to keep the dogs entertained. These touches can make a significant difference in how comfortable and happy the animals feel during their stay.

Maintaining cleanliness should be a top priority, so stocking up on cleaning supplies is essential. Disinfectants, pet-safe cleaning sprays, mops, and vacuum cleaners will help you maintain a spotless facility. A washing station or dog bath area can also come in handy for cleaning up after messy play or for offering grooming services. Keeping everything organized with labeled storage for supplies ensures that your staff can work efficiently and that nothing gets overlooked.

Safety equipment is another critical category to consider. First aid kits, leashes, and harnesses should always be readily available. In addition, having fire extinguishers, smoke detectors, and an evacuation plan in place will prepare you for emergencies. This not only protects the dogs but also ensures the safety of your staff and the facility itself. Clients will appreciate knowing that you take safety measures seriously, which builds trust and confidence in your business.

Finally, remember that running a dog boarding business isn't just about caring for the dogs—it's also about maintaining good relationships with their owners. Items like report cards, cameras for live updates, or even small treats for the owners to take home can leave a positive impression. By investing in the right equipment and supplies, you're not just setting up a facility; you're creating a welcoming space where dogs feel at ease and their owners feel reassured.

Essential Equipment

- Kennels or Suites: Provide secure, comfortable enclosures for overnight stays.
    - Feeding Stations: Stock food bowls and storage bins for pet food.
    - Cleaning Supplies: Include disinfectants, mops, and waste disposal equipment.
    - Leashes and Collars: Have extras for walking or managing dogs.
    - Bedding and Toys: Offer cozy bedding and toys to make dogs feel at home.

Additional Supplies

- Grooming tools like brushes, nail clippers, and shampoo.
    - First-aid kits for emergency care.
    - Surveillance cameras and monitoring systems for security.

Investing in quality equipment and supplies ensures a professional and well-maintained facility, which is crucial for customer satisfaction and repeat business.

—-

By carefully choosing a location, designing a functional and dog-friendly space, securing necessary permits, and equipping your facility, you'll create a strong foundation for your dog boarding business.

CHAPTER 4: LEGAL AND FINANCIAL CONSIDERATIONS

Starting and managing a business involves far more than just offering a service or product. Behind the scenes, there are essential legal and financial considerations that must be addressed to establish a strong foundation for success. Failing to properly navigate these areas can lead to costly mistakes, potential legal issues, or financial instability down the road. This chapter provides a roadmap for handling legal and financial matters effectively, ensuring that the groundwork for your venture is built on solid, sustainable practices. From choosing the right legal structure to setting up accounting systems, we'll explore the key steps that will help safeguard the business and keep operations running smoothly.

The first step in building a secure foundation is selecting the appropriate legal structure for your business. Whether you choose to operate as a sole proprietorship, partnership, LLC, or corporation, the right structure can impact everything from personal liability to tax obligations. This chapter will guide you through the different options, explaining the advantages and disadvantages of each, so you can make an informed decision that aligns with your business goals. Understanding the legal implications of your choice will help you avoid unnecessary risks and ensure that you're positioned for long-term success.

Once the legal structure is in place, attention must turn to the financial side of the business. A clear and detailed financial plan is essential for managing cash flow, expenses, and profits. This chapter will outline strategies for setting up your business's financial systems, including choosing the right accounting methods, tracking income and expenses, and ensuring tax compliance. With the right financial tools in place, you'll be able to monitor the health of your business and make informed decisions that support growth and sustainability.

Legal compliance also extends to important operational matters, such as obtaining necessary permits, licenses, and insurance. In this chapter, we'll discuss how to ensure your business is fully compliant with local, state, and federal regulations. We'll also explore the importance of business insurance in protecting your assets and mitigating risks, from liability coverage to workers' compensation. Understanding these legal obligations will give you peace of mind, knowing that your business is operating within the law and is protected from potential threats.

Finally, this chapter will cover the importance of contracts and agreements, both with clients and vendors, to clearly define expectations and minimize misunderstandings. From service agreements with clients to supplier contracts, having these documents in place is essential for protecting your business interests. We'll discuss how to draft clear, enforceable agreements and the role of legal counsel in reviewing contracts to ensure that they're in your best interest.

By the end of this chapter, you'll have a comprehensive understanding of the key legal and financial considerations that come with starting and managing a business. With this knowledge, you'll be equipped to make the right decisions, set up effective systems, and create a secure, compliant foundation that will support the growth and success of your venture for years to come.

—-

CHAPTER 4: LEGAL AND FINANCIAL CONSIDERATIONS

1. Registering Your Business

The first step in starting your dog boarding business is to legally register it. This process ensures that your business is recognized by the government and allows you to operate without legal complications. The requirements for registration vary depending on your location, so it's important to research local, state, and federal guidelines. One of the initial decisions you'll need to make is choosing your business structure, such as a sole proprietorship, partnership, limited liability company (LLC), or corporation. Each option comes with its own legal, tax, and financial implications, so take time to select the structure that best suits your needs and goals.

Once you've decided on the structure, you'll need to file the appropriate paperwork with the relevant authorities. For example, registering as an LLC typically involves submitting articles of organization and paying a filing fee. You'll also need to choose a name for your business, ensuring it's unique and adheres to any naming regulations in your area. In some cases, you may need to register a "Doing Business As" (DBA) name if you plan to operate under a different name than your registered entity. This step helps protect your brand and prevents other businesses from using the same name.

Obtaining a tax identification number (EIN) from the Internal Revenue Service (IRS) is another essential part of the registration process. This number is used for tax purposes and is necessary if you plan to hire employees or open a business bank account. For sole proprietors, it's sometimes optional, but having one can still simplify tax filings and other administrative tasks. Additionally, you may need to register for state and local taxes, depending on where your business operates.

After completing the formal registration process, it's important to acquire any additional licenses or permits required for dog boarding businesses in your area. This could include zoning permits, health department approvals, or kennel licenses. These permits ensure that your facility complies with local laws and provides a safe environment for the animals. Skipping these steps can lead to legal issues, fines, or even the closure of your business, so it's worth taking the time to get everything in order.

Registering your business is more than just a legal requirement—it's the foundation for your venture. A properly registered and licensed business signals to clients that you're professional, trustworthy, and serious about providing high-quality care for their pets. By getting this step right, you're setting yourself up for success and avoiding potential challenges down the road.

Steps to Register Your Business:

- Choose a Business Name: Select a unique and memorable name that reflects your brand. Check its availability to avoid trademark issues.
    - Select a Business Structure: Options include sole proprietorship, partnership, limited liability company (LLC), or corporation. Each has its pros and cons, including tax implications and liability protection.
    - File Necessary Documents: Depending on your structure, file the appropriate registration forms with your state or local government.
    - Obtain Licenses and Permits: Research and acquire the required licenses and permits specific to your industry and location.

—-

2. Understanding Zoning and Insurance Requirements

Before opening your dog boarding business, it's crucial to understand and comply with zoning regulations in your area. Zoning laws dictate where

CHAPTER 4: LEGAL AND FINANCIAL CONSIDERATIONS

specific types of businesses can operate and help maintain harmony within communities. For instance, some residential areas may not allow animal-related businesses due to noise or safety concerns. Contact your local zoning office to verify whether your chosen location is zoned for a dog boarding facility. In cases where it isn't, you may need to apply for a zoning variance or find a location better suited for your operations.

Aside from zoning, obtaining the right insurance is a critical step in safeguarding your business. General liability insurance is a must for any dog boarding business, as it protects you from claims related to accidents, injuries, or property damage. For example, if a dog in your care injures another dog or person, liability insurance can cover the associated costs. Similarly, property insurance can protect your facility and equipment from damage caused by fires, natural disasters, or theft. Having comprehensive coverage ensures that unexpected events don't jeopardize your business.

Another important type of insurance to consider is animal bailee insurance, which is specifically designed for businesses that handle other people's pets. This coverage helps protect you in the event of injury, illness, or loss of a pet while in your care. Given the emotional and financial value of pets, having this coverage can provide peace of mind for both you and your clients. Additionally, workers' compensation insurance is essential if you plan to hire employees, as it covers medical expenses and lost wages in case of workplace injuries.

Ensuring compliance with zoning laws and securing appropriate insurance not only protects your business but also builds credibility with clients. Pet owners want to know their furry friends are in safe hands, and demonstrating that you've taken all necessary legal and financial precautions can go a long way in earning their trust. Moreover, having proper insurance can save you from costly legal battles and provide support during unforeseen incidents, giving your business greater stability in the long run.

By addressing zoning and insurance requirements early on, you're setting a strong foundation for your business. These steps may seem tedious, but they are essential for ensuring smooth operations and protecting your investment. With these elements in place, you can focus on providing top-notch care for the dogs in your facility, knowing that your business is well-prepared to handle potential challenges.

Zoning Requirements:
- Check local zoning ordinances to ensure your business location is compliant.
- If you operate from home, verify whether a home-based business is allowed in your area.
- Apply for zoning variances if your business activities fall outside existing regulations.

Insurance Needs:
- General Liability Insurance: Covers accidents, injuries, and property damage.
- Professional Liability Insurance: Protects against claims of negligence or errors in service.
- Workers' Compensation Insurance: Mandatory if you have employees, providing coverage for work-related injuries.
- Property Insurance: Covers damages to your business premises and equipment.

—-

Pricing Your Services

Getting the pricing right for your services is one of the most critical aspects of running a business. It's not just about picking a number that feels right—

CHAPTER 4: LEGAL AND FINANCIAL CONSIDERATIONS

it's about finding that balance between earning a fair profit and offering something your customers feel is worth their money. If you price too high, you risk scaring people away. Price too low, and you might end up working hard without seeing the financial benefits you deserve. It's about understanding your value and how that aligns with what your audience is willing to pay.

To start, think about all the costs involved in delivering your services. This includes everything from materials and time to any extra expenses like tools or software. Once you have a clear picture of your expenses, it's easier to set a price that not only covers your costs but also gives you a profit. But don't stop there—consider the market as well. Look at what others in your industry are charging. Are their prices much higher or lower than what you had in mind? This step can help you decide if your pricing is realistic and competitive.

Another factor to think about is how your pricing reflects your brand. What message are you sending with your prices? Are you positioning yourself as a premium, high-quality service provider, or are you aiming for affordability and accessibility? The price you set tells people what to expect from your services, so it's important to make sure it matches the level of quality and experience you're offering. This doesn't mean you need to underprice yourself to attract customers. Instead, focus on making your value clear so customers understand why your price is justified.

Once you've settled on a price, be ready to adjust over time. As your skills grow or market conditions change, your pricing might need to evolve. Don't be afraid to raise your rates when necessary, especially if you're delivering more value than you were when you started. Sometimes, clients actually respect and trust you more when your pricing reflects confidence in the quality of your work. Of course, any changes should be communicated clearly and professionally, so your clients understand what they're paying for.

Finally, remember that pricing is not just a financial decision—it's a strategic one. It can affect how people perceive your services and whether they'll choose you over someone else. Take the time to figure out what works for both you and your clients. When done right, your pricing will support your business, build trust with your customers, and give you the confidence to grow in the long run.

Factors to Consider:
- Cost of Operations: Include expenses like supplies, rent, utilities, and salaries.
- Market Research: Study competitors' pricing to position yourself strategically.
- Value Proposition: Price your services based on the value you provide to customers.
- Profit Margin: Aim for a margin that sustains your business while being fair to clients.

Tips for Pricing:
- Start with introductory pricing to attract customers, then adjust as demand grows.
- Offer tiered pricing or packages for different customer needs.
- Regularly review and update prices based on inflation, demand, and market trends.

—-

Managing Taxes

Taxes are a part of life and an unavoidable aspect of running any business. While they might feel overwhelming at first, understanding and managing them properly is essential. Failing to meet your tax obligations can lead to

CHAPTER 4: LEGAL AND FINANCIAL CONSIDERATIONS

unnecessary stress, financial penalties, or even legal trouble. On the other hand, staying on top of your taxes keeps your finances in check and helps you avoid surprises down the road.

The first step is knowing what taxes apply to your business. Depending on where you live and the type of work you do, you might need to pay income tax, self-employment tax, sales tax, or other local and state taxes. Make it a point to research your obligations or consult a tax professional who can guide you through the process. Having the right information upfront makes things much easier when it comes time to file.

Keeping organized records is another key part of managing taxes. Save receipts, invoices, and any documents related to your business expenses and income. This doesn't just make tax filing smoother—it also helps you claim deductions and credits you're entitled to. These deductions, such as for home office expenses or equipment, can significantly reduce your tax bill. Use a system that works for you, whether it's digital tools or traditional files, so everything is easy to access when needed.

It's also wise to set aside money throughout the year to cover your taxes. Many small business owners make the mistake of waiting until the deadline, only to realize they don't have enough to pay what's owed. By setting aside a portion of your earnings regularly, you can avoid that last-minute scramble. If your income varies, consider using an estimated percentage to set aside money after each payment you receive.

Finally, don't hesitate to ask for help if taxes feel too complicated. Hiring an accountant or using reliable tax software can save you time and stress. These professionals and tools can help ensure you're meeting all legal requirements and taking advantage of every deduction available. Properly managing taxes might seem like a hassle, but it's an important part of running a successful business. When you stay informed and prepared, you can focus more on growing your business and less on worrying about tax deadlines.

Tax Responsibilities:
- Obtain a Tax ID: Register for a Tax Identification Number (TIN) or Employer Identification Number (EIN).
- Understand Tax Types: Learn about income tax, self-employment tax, sales tax, and payroll tax.
- Track Business Expenses: Maintain accurate records of all business-related expenses to maximize deductions.
- File on Time: Ensure you meet all tax deadlines to avoid penalties.

Tools for Tax Management:
- Use accounting software like QuickBooks or FreshBooks to streamline tax preparation.
- Hire a tax professional for expert advice and filing assistance.
- Stay informed about tax law changes that may affect your business.

—-

Key Takeaways:
- Legal and financial compliance lays the groundwork for a successful business.
- Registering your business, adhering to zoning laws, and obtaining insurance protect against legal risks.
- Thoughtful pricing and diligent tax management contribute to profitability and sustainability.

By addressing these considerations early and consistently, you'll establish a business that thrives on strong legal and financial foundations.

CHAPTER 5: DEVELOPING SERVICES AND PACKAGES

In today's competitive pet care industry, simply providing basic dog boarding services may no longer be enough to stand out. Pet owners are increasingly looking for more than just a place to keep their dogs while they're away—they want a comprehensive, personalized experience that caters to the unique needs of their pets. Offering a variety of services and customizable packages not only helps attract new clients but also plays a crucial role in retaining them for the long term. In this chapter, we will delve into the importance of developing a range of boarding services, incorporating additional offerings that add value, and creating personalized care plans that go beyond the basics.

When it comes to boarding, no two dogs are exactly alike. Some dogs may have special medical needs, while others may require extra playtime or more one-on-one attention to feel comfortable in a new environment. Understanding these unique needs and tailoring your services to address them is essential in building a reputation as a compassionate, high-quality pet care provider. It's not just about offering a place to sleep—it's about offering an experience that keeps pets happy, healthy, and safe, while giving owners peace of mind.

Creating a variety of service options ensures that you can cater to a diverse client base. Whether it's luxury accommodations for pampered pets, basic boarding for budget-conscious clients, or specialized care for dogs with medical conditions or behavioral challenges, offering multiple options allows you to meet the needs of every client. Customizable packages that allow owners to select add-ons—such as grooming, training, or extended playtime—give them the flexibility to design a care plan that aligns with their dog's personality, preferences, and health requirements.

The key to retaining clients is not only offering exceptional service but also providing a personalized experience. This chapter will also explore how to build personalized care plans that reflect each pet's individual needs. By taking the time to get to know your clients' pets and offering thoughtful recommendations, you can develop a relationship built on trust and understanding. From a dog's favorite toys and daily routines to its dietary preferences or fears, customizing their care ensures they feel comfortable and secure while staying at your facility. These personalized services not only create happy pets but also lead to satisfied owners who are more likely to return and recommend your business to others.

Additionally, we will discuss the importance of effective communication with pet owners to ensure that their expectations are met and exceeded. By being transparent about what's included in your services and keeping owners updated about their pets' well-being, you can create a relationship of mutual trust. When clients feel confident that their pets are receiving the best possible care, they are more likely to return, spread positive word-of-mouth, and become loyal customers.

In this chapter, we will also touch on the business side of offering a wide range of services. From pricing strategies to managing service packages, we'll discuss how to balance the needs of your clients with the operational realities of running a successful boarding facility. By diversifying your offerings and adding thoughtful, customized care plans, you can elevate your business, enhance customer satisfaction, and increase revenue potential.

CHAPTER 5: DEVELOPING SERVICES AND PACKAGES

In summary, the pet care industry is evolving, and dog boarding services must keep pace by offering a variety of services that cater to the individual needs of pets. This chapter will guide you through the process of building a flexible, customer-focused service offering that will set your business apart and help you build long-lasting relationships with your clients. Whether you're just starting out or looking to expand your current offerings, the strategies explored here will help you create a thriving business that keeps both pets and their owners happy.

—-

1. Types of Boarding Services

Pet boarding services should cater to a wide range of client needs, from basic care to premium options.

Common Types of Boarding Services:
  - Standard Boarding: Includes basic care such as feeding, exercise, and a clean sleeping area. Ideal for short-term stays.
  - Luxury Boarding: Offers premium amenities like private suites, plush bedding, and webcams for owners to check on their pets.
  - Medical Boarding: Designed for pets with special medical needs, staffed with trained professionals to administer medication or monitor health conditions.
  - Day Boarding: For clients who need daytime care while at work. Focuses on exercise, socialization, and basic needs.

Tips for Success:
  - Ensure all boarding areas are clean, secure, and comfortable.
  - Maintain a low staff-to-pet ratio for personalized attention.
  - Establish clear policies on vaccinations and health requirements to ensure a safe environment.

—-

Additional Offerings (e.g., Grooming, Training)

Expanding your business to include additional services is an effective way to increase value for your customers and set yourself apart from competitors. Whether it's offering grooming services, training, or other related offerings, it gives people more reasons to choose your business and stay loyal. By diversifying your offerings, you can also attract a wider audience who may have specific needs that your primary service doesn't cover. This not only helps boost your revenue but also strengthens your brand's reputation as a one-stop shop.

For example, if you're in the pet care industry, adding grooming services to your business can provide convenience for pet owners who prefer to handle multiple needs in one place. If you're running a fitness business, offering personalized training sessions alongside group classes can cater to individuals who require more specialized attention. These additional services enhance the overall experience for your customers, making them more likely to return and recommend you to others.

Offering extras can also help you stand out in a crowded market. Many businesses stick to one core service, which can be limiting in terms of growth. But by adding complementary services, you provide more value that appeals to both new and existing customers. If you can solve more problems for your clients, they're less likely to shop around for alternatives. This strengthens the relationship you have with them and builds customer loyalty.

While adding extra services is beneficial, it's important to ensure they align with your brand and expertise. For example, if you're a pet trainer, offering grooming might feel like a natural fit. But if you're a personal trainer, it's crucial to stay within your area of expertise when adding services like nutrition coaching or recovery sessions. This helps maintain your reputation for quality and ensures you can deliver on the promises you make to your clients.

CHAPTER 5: DEVELOPING SERVICES AND PACKAGES

Lastly, think about how to price these additional services. While they should be priced competitively, they should also reflect the quality you provide. Packaging services together at a discount, offering bundles, or providing loyalty perks for customers who regularly use multiple services can be effective ways to encourage more purchases. By carefully selecting and pricing your extra services, you'll attract more customers, increase satisfaction, and create new opportunities for growth.

Popular Additional Services:
 - Grooming Services: Bathing, nail trimming, haircuts, and other grooming options can be offered as add-ons or standalone services.
 - Training Programs: Provide obedience training, behavioral coaching, or specialized programs like agility training.
 - Pet Transportation: Offer pick-up and drop-off services for added convenience.
 - Enrichment Activities: Include puzzle games, group play sessions, or one-on-one time with a staff member to keep pets mentally and physically stimulated.

Benefits of Additional Offerings:
 - Increases revenue by providing more options for clients.
 - Strengthens customer loyalty by meeting multiple needs in one place.
 - Positions your business as a one-stop solution for pet care.

—-

Creating Customized Care Plans for Clients

In the competitive pet care industry, personalization is a key factor that can help your business stand out. Pet owners want to feel confident that their pets are receiving care that is tailored to their unique needs. By offering customized care plans, you show clients that you take the time to understand their pets' individual requirements, preferences, and health concerns. This personal touch not only strengthens the bond between you and your clients but also helps build trust, making them more likely to return and recommend your services.

To begin creating customized care plans, it's essential to gather detailed information about each pet. This could include their breed, age, medical history, temperament, and any specific behavior concerns. For instance, a pet with special dietary needs, chronic health conditions, or anxiety may require different attention compared to a healthy, high-energy dog. By learning these details upfront, you can offer services like tailored grooming schedules, special diets, or behavioral training that best suit each pet's needs.

Incorporating flexibility into your care plans is another important aspect of personalization. Some pets might respond better to specific grooming techniques, while others may prefer certain activities or need more downtime between services. Understanding these preferences allows you to adjust your approach, ensuring the pet's comfort and happiness. For example, if a dog is particularly nervous about baths, you could incorporate calming treatments or a more gentle bathing process. Small adjustments like these show clients that you are truly invested in their pets' well-being.

Another benefit of creating personalized care plans is that it enables you to offer more comprehensive services. By understanding a pet's unique needs, you can suggest additional services that might benefit them, such as specific training, behavioral support, or even health monitoring. This not only adds value to your offerings but also creates a sense of continuity in the pet's care. For example, a dog undergoing behavioral training might also benefit from grooming sessions that reinforce positive behavior, leading to a well-rounded care experience.

Lastly, personalized care plans can be a powerful marketing tool. When potential clients see that you offer services tailored to their pet's individual needs, they're more likely to choose you over competitors. You can highlight

CHAPTER 5: DEVELOPING SERVICES AND PACKAGES

these plans on your website or in your promotional materials, emphasizing how you take the time to get to know each pet and cater to their specific needs. As word spreads, your reputation for providing thoughtful, customized care will help you attract and retain loyal customers in the long run.

Steps to Create Customized Care Plans:

1. Initial Consultation: Meet with clients to understand their pet's unique needs, preferences, and health requirements.

2. Detailed Questionnaires: Use forms to gather information on diet, exercise routines, medical history, and behavioral tendencies.

3. Tailored Services: Based on the information, offer personalized feeding schedules, playtime routines, or grooming preferences.

4. Ongoing Communication: Provide regular updates to pet owners, including photos, videos, or reports on their pet's stay.

Examples of Customization:
- A senior dog might require softer bedding, slower-paced activities, and medication management.
- An energetic puppy might benefit from extra play sessions, socialization, and training reinforcement.

Benefits of Custom Care Plans:
- Builds trust and rapport with clients.
- Improves pet satisfaction and well-being.
- Encourages repeat business and word-of-mouth referrals.

—-

Key Takeaways
- Diversify your services to attract a wide range of clients, from basic boarding to luxury options.
- Additional offerings like grooming and training add value and convenience for pet owners.

- Customizing care plans demonstrates your commitment to meeting individual client needs and can set your business apart from competitors.

By thoughtfully developing your services and packages, you'll create a business that prioritizes the well-being of pets while exceeding client expectations.

CHAPTER 6: MARKETING AND BRANDING YOUR BUSINESS

In today's fast-paced and highly competitive pet care industry, effective marketing and branding are not just important—they're essential. A well-crafted marketing strategy helps you stand out from the crowd, attracts new clients, and builds a loyal customer base. However, it's not just about advertising your services; it's about creating a lasting impression that reflects your values, professionalism, and dedication to pets and their owners. In this chapter, we'll explore the importance of building a strong brand identity and delve into actionable strategies for marketing your pet care business in both the digital world and your local community.

The foundation of a successful marketing strategy begins with a strong brand. Your brand is more than just a logo or catchy tagline; it's the overall image and reputation that clients associate with your business. Whether it's the compassionate care you provide, the level of professionalism your staff maintains, or the specialized services you offer, your brand should reflect what sets you apart from the competition. Developing a clear brand message, from your business's core values to your target audience, will help guide all your marketing efforts and ensure consistency in the way clients perceive your business.

One of the most powerful tools for reaching potential clients today is an online presence. With more people than ever turning to the internet to search for pet care services, a user-friendly, visually appealing website is a must-have. But simply having a website is not enough. We'll discuss how to optimize your site for search engines (SEO) so potential clients can easily find you online, and how to create engaging content that showcases your expertise and highlights the unique features of your services. In addition to your website, social media platforms like Facebook, Instagram, and Google My Business offer great opportunities to engage with your audience and build brand awareness. From sharing photos of happy pets to running special promotions, your online presence allows you to connect directly with your community and potential clients in a way that feels personal and authentic.

While online marketing is critical, local advertising still plays a significant role in attracting clients, especially for businesses like pet care facilities that thrive on community relationships. This chapter will cover strategies for effective local advertising, from partnering with other businesses in the area to running promotions or hosting events that get people talking. Whether it's creating flyers for local vet clinics, sponsoring community events, or offering discounts for first-time clients, local advertising helps you connect with pet owners right where they live. A strong local presence fosters a sense of community and trust that can turn one-time clients into repeat customers.

Building partnerships with local veterinarians, pet stores, and other pet-related businesses is another key strategy for marketing your pet care business. These relationships can lead to valuable referrals, allowing you to tap into an established network of pet owners who are already seeking out trusted services for their pets. We'll explore how to approach potential partners, build mutually beneficial relationships, and create referral programs that incentivize collaboration. By aligning yourself with other reputable businesses in the pet care space, you increase your credibility and expand your reach.

Finally, we'll discuss the importance of gathering and using client feedback to refine your marketing efforts. Positive reviews, testimonials, and word-of-mouth recommendations are powerful tools that can amplify your marketing efforts. We'll cover best practices for requesting reviews, responding to customer feedback, and turning satisfied clients into your best advocates. When you take the time to build genuine relationships with your clients, their loyalty and support can be one of the most effective marketing strategies available to you.

In this chapter, you'll learn how to build an effective marketing plan that encompasses both digital and local strategies, helping you create a brand that resonates with your target audience and drives business growth. Whether you're just starting out or looking to refresh your current marketing efforts, these actionable strategies will guide you toward building a strong, recognizable presence in the pet care industry that attracts clients and establishes a loyal customer base. With the right approach to marketing and branding, you can elevate your business and ensure long-term success in this ever-growing industry.

—-

Building an Online Presence

In today's digital world, having a strong online presence is essential for growing your business. The internet is often the first place potential clients will look when they need services, and it's where they'll form their first impression of your brand. Your website and social media platforms are powerful tools that can help you reach a broader audience and engage with clients in a meaningful way. Without an effective online presence, you may miss out on valuable opportunities to connect with new customers and grow your business.

A well-designed website is the cornerstone of your online presence. It serves as your digital storefront and should clearly communicate who you are, what services you offer, and why potential clients should choose you. Make sure your website is easy to navigate, mobile-friendly, and visually appealing. Include clear calls to action, like booking appointments or contacting you for more information, so visitors know exactly how to take the next step. Additionally, showcase testimonials, client reviews, and any credentials or certifications you have, as these can help build trust with visitors.

Social media is another crucial aspect of building your online presence. Platforms like Facebook, Instagram, and Twitter allow you to interact directly with your audience and showcase your business in real-time. Share valuable content such as tips, behind-the-scenes looks at your services, and before-and-after photos of your work. Regularly engaging with followers through comments, messages, and posts helps humanize your brand and fosters a sense of community. The more active and engaging your social media presence, the more likely clients are to trust you and consider your services.

To really stand out, consider using digital marketing strategies to boost your online visibility. Search engine optimization (SEO) is one of the most effective ways to ensure your website appears in search results when potential clients are looking for your services. You can optimize your website by including relevant keywords, creating blog content, and ensuring that your site is technically sound. Paid advertising, such as Google Ads or social media ads, can also help target specific audiences and bring in new clients. These strategies can be especially helpful in a competitive market.

Finally, consistency is key to maintaining a strong online presence. Whether it's the tone of your website copy, the frequency of your social media posts, or the quality of your online customer service, consistency helps reinforce your brand identity and keeps your business top of mind for clients. In an increasingly digital world, an active and well-managed online presence can give you the edge you need to attract new clients and grow your business.

CHAPTER 6: MARKETING AND BRANDING YOUR BUSINESS

Steps to Build an Online Presence:
  - Create a Professional Website:
  - Include essential information: services, pricing, location, and contact details.
  - Use high-quality images of your facilities and happy pets.
  - Add client testimonials and success stories.
  - Incorporate a booking system for convenience.

- Leverage Social Media Platforms:
  - Post regularly on platforms like Instagram, Facebook, and TikTok.
  - Share engaging content, such as pet care tips, client pet spotlights, and behind-the-scenes glimpses of your business.
  - Respond promptly to comments and messages to build trust and engagement.

- Optimize for Search Engines (SEO):
  - Use relevant keywords like "pet boarding near me" or "dog grooming services."
  - Start a blog with topics like pet care advice or tips for choosing a boarding facility.
  - Register your business on Google My Business to appear in local searches.

—-

Local Advertising Tactics

Reaching out to your local community is one of the most effective ways to attract new customers and grow your business. When your services are geographically focused, connecting with people nearby is crucial for building a loyal client base. Local advertising allows you to engage directly with potential customers in your area, making them more likely to choose your business because they see you as accessible and involved in the community.

One of the best ways to advertise locally is through traditional methods like flyers, posters, and direct mail. These materials can be placed in local businesses, coffee shops, or community centers where people frequently visit. Make sure your promotional material is eye-catching and includes essential information such as your services, location, website, and contact details. Offering discounts or specials for first-time customers can also be an effective way to encourage people to try your services.

Another great tactic is partnering with other local businesses. Teaming up with businesses that have a similar target audience can help both of you reach more customers. For instance, if you run a pet care service, partnering with a local pet store, grooming salon, or veterinary clinic could be beneficial. You could cross-promote each other's services through flyers, social media shoutouts, or joint events. These partnerships allow you to tap into a pool of potential customers who already trust the businesses you're partnering with.

Participating in local events and sponsorships is another excellent way to get your name out there. Many communities host fairs, festivals, charity events, or local sports games, and sponsoring or volunteering at these events can provide valuable exposure. Setting up a booth or offering free services or samples can attract people who may not have heard of your business before. Additionally, being involved in local charity work or community initiatives helps build goodwill, which can translate into customer loyalty.

Finally, don't underestimate the power of word-of-mouth marketing. Encourage satisfied clients to recommend your services to their friends and family. Offering referral bonuses or discounts for each new customer they bring in can incentivize them to spread the word. Online review platforms like Google Reviews or Yelp also play a big role in attracting local clients. Positive reviews from people in your area can boost your credibility and make others feel more comfortable choosing your business. By focusing on local advertising, you not only draw in new customers but also build a reputation as a trusted, community-oriented business.

Effective Local Advertising Methods:
  - Flyers and Posters: Place them in high-traffic areas like parks, cafes, and community centers.
  - Local Events: Sponsor or participate in events like pet adoption drives or charity walks. Set up a booth to showcase your services.
  - Local Newspapers and Magazines: Advertise in print publications that target your area.
  - Direct Mail Campaigns: Send postcards or brochures to homes in your community, offering introductory discounts or promotions.

Word of Mouth:
Encourage satisfied clients to spread the word. Offer referral discounts to reward clients who bring in new customers.

—-

Building Relationships with Veterinarians and Pet Stores

Forming partnerships with local veterinarians and pet stores can be a game-changer for your pet care business. These professionals are often the first point of contact for pet owners when they need services or products for their pets, so building strong relationships with them can lead to a steady stream of referrals. By working together, you can establish credibility in the pet care community and gain access to a wider audience who trusts the recommendations of these local experts.

One of the simplest ways to start building relationships with veterinarians and pet stores is by introducing yourself and your services. Take the time to visit these businesses in person and provide them with information about what you offer. Offering complimentary services, such as a free consultation or a discount for first-time clients, can encourage these businesses to refer their customers to you. Veterinarians may appreciate knowing that you are available to help with post-surgery care, grooming, or training, while pet stores might refer you when customers are looking for additional services for their pets beyond what they can offer.

In addition to offering your services, consider collaborating with local veterinarians and pet stores on joint promotions or events. For example, you could host a "Pet Wellness Day" at a local pet store where you offer free pet assessments or grooming services, while the pet store offers discounts on products. Alternatively, veterinarians could refer clients to your business for specific care needs, and you could reciprocate by recommending their services to your clients. These collaborations not only help drive business to both parties but also create a sense of community and mutual support.

Another key benefit of these partnerships is the trust factor. When a veterinarian or pet store recommends your services, it provides immediate credibility with their clients. Pet owners are often very particular about who they trust with their pets, and a referral from a trusted source can make all the difference. Make sure you maintain a high standard of care and professionalism so that veterinarians and pet stores feel confident referring their clients to you. This helps build a long-term, trusted relationship that benefits both your business and theirs.

Finally, keeping in touch with these partners is crucial to sustaining a productive relationship. Regularly check in with local veterinarians and pet stores, keeping them updated on any new services or promotions you're offering. You can also send thank-you notes or small tokens of appreciation for their support. By nurturing these partnerships and consistently delivering excellent service, you can establish a strong reputation in the pet care community and continue to receive valuable referrals.

How to Build Relationships:
  - Connect with Veterinarians:
  - Introduce yourself and your services.
  - Provide brochures or business cards for them to share with their clients.
  - Offer special discounts for referrals from their clinic.

- Collaborate with Pet Stores:
  - Host joint events, such as pet care workshops or meet-and-greets.
  - Display your marketing materials in their store.
  - Partner on promotions, like offering discounts for their customers who book your services.

- Join Local Pet Communities:
  - Become active in pet-related social groups or online forums.
  - Attend or sponsor local pet meetups to network with other pet professionals.

—-

Key Takeaways

- A strong online presence enhances visibility and credibility. Invest in a professional website and actively engage on social media.
  - Local advertising builds awareness and attracts nearby clients. Utilize community events and print marketing to your advantage.
  - Building relationships with veterinarians and pet stores fosters valuable partnerships and referral opportunities.

By combining digital strategies with local outreach, you can effectively market your business and create a brand that resonates with pet owners in your community.

CHAPTER 7: DAY-TO-DAY OPERATIONS

Running a successful pet care business requires more than just a passion for animals—it demands strong operational management, attention to detail, and the ability to deliver exceptional service day in and day out. As a pet care provider, you're responsible for not only ensuring the well-being of the animals under your care but also making sure your clients feel confident and satisfied with the services you offer. Efficient management of daily tasks, from booking appointments to handling emergencies, is key to maintaining smooth operations and fostering long-term relationships with clients. In this chapter, we'll explore practical strategies for handling bookings, maintaining consistent pet care routines, managing unexpected situations, and exceeding customer expectations to build a thriving, well-run business.

One of the first steps in running a successful pet care business is streamlining your booking system. Whether you're offering dog boarding, daycare, grooming, or training services, having an organized and efficient system for managing client reservations is crucial to ensure that everything runs smoothly. A user-friendly online booking system can make scheduling appointments easy for clients, while reducing the workload on your staff. Additionally, an automated confirmation and reminder system helps reduce no-shows and keeps everyone on the same page. We'll discuss the importance of managing your bookings effectively, setting clear policies on cancellations and late arrivals, and ensuring that you always have the capacity to meet client demand without overbooking or overextending your resources.

Pet care routines are the backbone of your service, and maintaining consistency is essential for the health and happiness of the animals in your care. This includes everything from feeding schedules and exercise routines to grooming and medical needs. Establishing clear guidelines for how pets are cared for—based on their specific needs and preferences—ensures a high standard of care and reduces the likelihood of errors. In this chapter, we'll look at how to create detailed care plans for each pet, set up checklists for staff to follow, and monitor the pets' health and behavior closely. A well-maintained routine not only ensures that pets are happy and healthy but also creates a sense of trust and reliability among clients, knowing that their pets are in safe hands.

Emergencies are an inevitable part of running a pet care business, whether it's a sudden illness, injury, or a natural disaster. Being prepared to handle these situations calmly and effectively is critical to ensuring the safety and well-being of both the animals and your staff. Having emergency protocols in place, such as knowing where the nearest veterinary clinic is, having first aid kits readily available, and training staff on how to respond to common emergencies, can make a significant difference in how well your facility handles crises. We'll explore how to develop and communicate these protocols to your team, how to manage client expectations during emergencies, and how to handle stressful situations with professionalism and compassion.

Exceeding customer expectations is one of the most powerful ways to build a loyal client base. While it's important to meet the basic needs of your clients, going above and beyond in your service can leave a lasting impression that leads to repeat business and referrals. This could include personalized services, such as sending pet owners updates and photos of their pets during their stay, offering flexible scheduling options, or providing extra attention to pets with special needs. We'll explore how to foster a customer-first mentality, how to actively listen to client feedback, and how to continuously improve your services to ensure that clients feel valued and appreciated. Exceeding expectations doesn't have to mean offering extravagant extras—it's often the small, thoughtful gestures that make a big impact.

In this chapter, you'll gain insights into how to balance the day-to-day demands of running a pet care business with the goal of delivering exceptional care and service. Whether you're managing bookings, maintaining pet routines, handling emergencies, or going above and beyond for your clients, the strategies covered here will help you build a business that is efficient, organized, and customer-focused. By mastering these operational tasks and consistently delivering high-quality care, you can ensure that your pet care business runs smoothly, meets client expectations, and continues to grow and thrive.

—-

Managing Bookings and Schedules

An efficient and well-organized booking system is crucial for ensuring the smooth operation of your business. Whether you're offering pet care services, grooming, training, or any other service, keeping track of appointments, availability, and client preferences is key to maintaining customer satisfaction and maximizing your capacity. A disorganized booking process can lead to confusion, missed opportunities, and dissatisfied clients.

The first step in managing bookings effectively is to choose a system that suits your needs. Whether it's a physical appointment book, an online scheduling platform, or a specialized app, make sure it aligns with your business size and the type of services you offer. Online booking systems are often the most convenient for both you and your clients, as they allow clients to schedule appointments at their convenience and automatically update your calendar. This reduces the chance of double-booking or missed appointments.

In addition to basic scheduling, a good system should allow you to track client details and service history. For example, if you run a pet care business, knowing which pets are due for grooming, which need special treatments, or which ones have recurring appointments can help you plan your day more efficiently. By having this information at your fingertips, you can tailor your services to each client's needs, providing a more personalized experience and minimizing time spent on administrative tasks.

It's also important to implement policies for cancellations, rescheduling, and no-shows. Clear communication about your policies upfront can help clients understand the process and reduce scheduling conflicts. Consider sending reminders via text or email a day or two before appointments to reduce the chances of last-minute cancellations. Additionally, offering an easy way for clients to reschedule their appointments can help them stay on track without disrupting your schedule.

Lastly, keep an eye on your capacity and manage your time wisely. Overbooking can lead to burnout and lower the quality of your services, while underbooking can result in lost revenue. By regularly reviewing your schedule and adjusting your offerings, you can strike a balance between maintaining a healthy workload and maximizing the number of appointments you can handle each day. With an organized and effective booking system in place, you can ensure smooth operations, boost customer satisfaction, and increase your business's overall efficiency.

Tips for Managing Bookings:
  - Use Booking Software: Invest in software that allows clients to make reservations online and tracks availability in real time. Examples include Gingr, PetExec, or a custom-built system.

- Create a Scheduling Protocol: Maintain a clear schedule for feeding, exercise, grooming, and pick-up/drop-off times.
- Confirm Details: Before the stay, confirm all booking details, including dates, special requests, and vaccination records.
- Maintain a Waitlist: In peak seasons, keep a waitlist to fill last-minute cancellations efficiently.

Communication is Key:
   - Send reminders to clients about upcoming bookings.
   - Keep them updated during their pet's stay with photos or short messages.

—-

Feeding, Cleaning, and Exercising Dogs

Providing proper care for dogs is the heart of any pet care business. Dogs, like people, thrive on routine and consistency, so ensuring that feeding, cleaning, and exercise are part of their daily care plan is essential. By focusing on these key areas and paying attention to the specific needs of each dog, you can create a positive and nurturing environment that promotes both physical and emotional well-being.

Feeding dogs properly involves not just providing the right type of food, but also ensuring they are fed at the right times and in appropriate amounts. Each dog has its own dietary needs depending on its breed, age, size, and health condition. Consistently following these feeding guidelines helps maintain their health and energy levels. It's important to track what each dog eats and any special dietary restrictions or preferences they may have, ensuring that meals are prepared and served according to their individual needs. This attention to detail not only keeps the dogs healthy but also helps build trust with their owners, who will appreciate the care you provide.

Cleaning is another crucial aspect of daily pet care. Dogs require regular grooming to keep their coats healthy, their skin free from irritation, and to reduce shedding. Whether it's brushing, bathing, or nail trimming, establishing a consistent grooming routine ensures dogs stay clean and comfortable. For dogs that require specific treatments, such as skin care or flea control, paying attention to these extra steps can prevent health issues and enhance their overall well-being. Keeping the dogs' living space clean is equally important—daily cleaning of bedding, toys, and food areas ensures a hygienic environment and reduces the risk of infections or pests.

Exercise is essential for a dog's physical and mental health. Regular exercise helps keep dogs fit, reduce anxiety, and prevent behavioral problems. Depending on the dog's breed and energy level, the type and duration of exercise will vary. Some dogs may need long walks, while others may benefit from shorter, more intense play sessions. It's important to maintain a consistent exercise routine and adjust it based on the dog's age, health, and activity level. Regular outdoor time not only promotes health but also provides dogs with much-needed stimulation and the opportunity to socialize, which is essential for their emotional well-being.

By consistently prioritizing feeding, cleaning, and exercising dogs, you create a well-rounded and effective care routine that benefits both the dogs and their owners. Attention to these details builds trust with clients and strengthens the reputation of your pet care business. Providing reliable, compassionate care on a daily basis ensures that dogs stay happy, healthy, and well-cared for, leading to satisfied clients and a thriving business.

Feeding:
   - Follow specific feeding instructions provided by pet owners.
   - Maintain a feeding schedule to avoid disruptions to the pet's routine.
   - Monitor pets during mealtime to ensure safety, especially in group settings.

Cleaning:
- Clean and sanitize sleeping areas, food bowls, and toys daily to maintain hygiene.
- Use pet-safe cleaning products to avoid harmful chemicals.
- Regularly inspect and address any maintenance issues in your facility.

Exercising:
- Provide regular exercise tailored to each pet's energy level and health needs.
- Offer a mix of activities, such as walks, play sessions, or agility exercises.
- Ensure all pets are supervised during outdoor activities to prevent accidents.

—-

Handling Emergencies

Handling emergencies is an essential part of running a pet care business, as it ensures both the safety of the pets in your care and the peace of mind of their owners. Emergencies can arise at any time, whether it's a sudden health issue, an injury, or a pet behaving unpredictably. Being prepared for these situations can make a significant difference in how you respond and how quickly the issue is addressed, which can prevent further harm and ensure the well-being of the animals you care for.

The first step in handling emergencies is ensuring that you and your staff are well-trained in basic pet first aid and CPR. Knowing how to respond to common emergencies, such as choking, poisoning, or cuts and scrapes, can save a pet's life. Consider taking courses or certifications in pet first aid and emergency care, and make sure everyone involved in caring for the animals is trained to handle such situations calmly and effectively. Keeping a first aid kit stocked with necessary supplies is also a must, as it ensures you're prepared to treat minor injuries and stabilize pets until they can receive professional medical attention.

Equally important is knowing when to involve a veterinarian. In some cases, a situation may require more specialized care than you can provide. Having a list of trusted local veterinarians and emergency animal clinics readily available, along with clear procedures for transporting pets in case of an emergency, ensures that you can act swiftly if necessary. Informing clients about your emergency protocol in advance—such as what steps you will take if their pet is injured or falls ill—also helps them feel confident in the care you provide.

Communication is key during emergencies. If something goes wrong, it's important to immediately notify the pet's owner. Keeping them informed about the situation, whether it's an accident or a health issue, allows them to make any necessary decisions for their pet's well-being. Transparency and promptness in communication can ease their worries and demonstrate that you're handling the situation responsibly. Additionally, it's a good idea to keep detailed records of any emergency situations, including the actions you took and any veterinary interventions, so that the pet owner has a clear understanding of what happened.

Finally, taking steps to prevent emergencies in the first place can help minimize risk. Regularly checking pet facilities, ensuring that the animals are kept in safe environments, and maintaining up-to-date health records for each pet all contribute to a lower risk of emergencies. Preventive care is just as important as how you respond when something goes wrong. Being proactive and prepared not only helps protect the pets in your care but also strengthens your reputation as a responsible and reliable pet care provider.

Emergency Protocols:
  - Health Emergencies: Keep a list of nearby veterinarians and emergency

clinics. Ensure all staff are trained in basic pet first aid.

- Behavioral Issues: Have a plan for handling aggressive or overly anxious pets, such as separate holding areas or calming techniques.

- Natural Disasters: Develop an evacuation plan in case of fires, floods, or other emergencies. Communicate the plan to staff and practice drills regularly.

Proactive Measures:

- Require clients to provide emergency contact information and a list of medical conditions or special needs.

- Keep an emergency kit on hand with essentials like bandages, antiseptics, and a pet first aid guide.

—-

Ensuring Customer Satisfaction

Ensuring customer satisfaction is crucial to the success of any business, and in the pet care industry, happy clients can become your best advocates. When pet owners feel that their pets are being cared for with attention, respect, and professionalism, they are more likely to return and recommend your services to others. Going above and beyond in every interaction, from the first inquiry to the follow-up after services are rendered, is key to building lasting relationships with your customers and growing your business.

One of the most important aspects of customer satisfaction is clear and consistent communication. Be responsive to inquiries, whether they come through phone calls, emails, or social media, and always provide accurate information. Pet owners want to feel heard and valued, so take the time to listen to their concerns or requests about their pets' care. Whether it's about a grooming preference or special instructions for feeding or exercise, paying attention to the details can make a big difference in how clients perceive your service. Setting clear expectations and being transparent about your processes also helps build trust and minimizes misunderstandings.

Additionally, providing personalized care for each pet and their owner enhances satisfaction. Every pet is unique, and pet owners appreciate when you take the time to understand their pet's specific needs, whether it's a medical condition, anxiety triggers, or special care routines. Offering tailored services based on these details shows that you genuinely care about their pet's well-being and are dedicated to providing high-quality care. Regularly checking in with clients about their pets' experiences also helps you stay on top of any changes or preferences, allowing you to adjust your services accordingly.

Follow-up is another essential part of ensuring customer satisfaction. After a service, reach out to your clients to check if they were happy with the care their pet received. This can be a simple thank-you message or a request for feedback. Not only does this show that you care about their experience, but it also gives clients an opportunity to share their thoughts and provide constructive feedback. If any issues arise, addressing them promptly and professionally can help turn a potentially negative experience into a positive one, showing your commitment to making things right.

Finally, exceeding expectations is a powerful way to create loyal customers who are likely to spread the word about your business. Small gestures like offering a free service after a few visits, sending pet care tips, or remembering a pet's birthday can go a long way in making clients feel appreciated. When customers feel that you are going above and beyond for their pets, they will not only continue to use your services but will also recommend you to friends and family. By consistently striving to exceed expectations in every interaction, you can ensure that your clients are not only satisfied but are also excited to share their positive experiences with others.

CHAPTER 7: DAY-TO-DAY OPERATIONS

Tips for Building Customer Loyalty:

- Provide Regular Updates: Send daily updates with photos or videos of their pets. This reassures clients and shows your commitment to care.
- Offer Extras: Surprise clients with small gestures, like a personalized note or a complimentary service during their pet's stay.
- Seek Feedback: Encourage clients to share their experience and use the insights to improve your services.
- Address Complaints Quickly: Resolve issues promptly and professionally to maintain trust.

Create a Welcoming Experience:

- Ensure check-ins and check-outs are seamless. Have all paperwork ready in advance.
- Greet every client warmly and thank them for choosing your services.

—-

Key Takeaways

- Efficient booking and scheduling systems ensure smooth daily operations.
- Prioritizing pet care through feeding, cleaning, and exercise fosters trust and satisfaction.
- Preparedness for emergencies safeguards pets and reassures owners.
- Exceptional customer service builds loyalty and strengthens your business reputation.

By managing daily tasks with care and professionalism, you can create an environment that pets love and clients recommend enthusiastically.

CHAPTER 8: HIRING AND TRAINING STAFF

As my pet care business grows, one of the most crucial steps I'll face is expanding my team. Hiring the right people and providing them with the right training isn't just about filling positions—it's about maintaining the high level of care and service that clients expect while creating a positive and engaging workplace for my staff. I understand that finding the right team members is key to ensuring the animals in my care are treated with the same love and respect that I would give them myself. In this chapter, I'll explore the process of deciding when it's time to hire, how to train staff effectively to uphold quality pet care, and how to foster a supportive work environment that helps my team thrive.

I know from experience that bringing on new team members can feel like both an exciting and daunting task. Whether I'm hiring for a new facility or expanding an existing team, there's a careful balance between growth and maintaining the quality that my clients expect. It's important to recognize when I need to hire—whether it's due to an increase in bookings, the introduction of new services, or the need for additional support. I'll dive into the signs that indicate it's time to bring in new people and how I can assess whether the current workload is sustainable. Recognizing these signs early on can prevent burnout and ensure that my team is never overwhelmed.

Training my team is where the real work begins. I want to make sure my staff

CHAPTER 8: HIRING AND TRAINING STAFF

has the knowledge and skills to provide the best care for the pets entrusted to me. I'll discuss how to develop a comprehensive training program that covers everything from the basics of pet care to emergency protocols and client communication. Training is not a one-time event—it's an ongoing process. I'll explore how I can create opportunities for continuous learning and development, whether it's through workshops, mentorship, or cross-training to ensure my staff is well-rounded and equipped to handle a variety of situations.

I believe that a positive, supportive work environment is essential for both employee retention and the overall success of my business. When my team feels valued and supported, they're more likely to deliver exceptional care to the pets and communicate more effectively with clients. In this chapter, I'll cover strategies for creating a workplace culture that promotes open communication, collaboration, and mutual respect. I'll share ideas on how to provide regular feedback, recognize achievements, and offer incentives that motivate my staff. A positive environment leads to happier employees, which ultimately results in a higher standard of service and a more enjoyable experience for both pets and owners.

Expanding my team is an exciting part of growing my pet care business. By making thoughtful decisions about when and how to hire, developing a thorough training process, and creating a supportive and engaging workplace, I can ensure that my team is equipped to provide top-tier service while fostering a positive environment. The strategies discussed in this chapter will help me not only maintain the high level of care my clients expect but also create a workplace where my team can grow, succeed, and feel appreciated. With the right team in place, I can confidently move forward and continue to grow my business while providing exceptional care to the pets who need it most.

—-

When to Hire Help

Recognizing when to hire help is a key decision in running a successful business. Whether you're managing a pet care service, a retail store, or any other type of service-based business, there comes a time when doing everything yourself can no longer sustain the quality of your operations. Hiring help at the right time ensures that you can continue to meet the needs of your clients while also preventing burnout and maintaining a healthy work-life balance.

One of the first signs that it may be time to bring in additional staff is when you consistently find yourself overwhelmed with tasks. If you're spending more time managing day-to-day operations, responding to emails, handling bookings, or doing administrative work than actually serving your clients or caring for the pets, it may be time to delegate. When you're stretched too thin, the quality of your service can start to suffer, and it can become difficult to meet the expectations of your clients. Hiring someone to help with administrative tasks, customer service, or other non-specialized duties allows you to focus on what you do best.

Another indicator that it's time to hire help is when you experience a significant increase in demand for your services. As your business grows, you may find that you're receiving more inquiries, bookings, or customers than you can handle alone. Rather than turning away clients or compromising service quality, bringing in additional staff can ensure that you continue to meet demand without sacrificing the level of care or attention that your customers expect. Hiring extra hands allows you to scale your business while maintaining efficiency.

Burnout is also a major consideration. If you're constantly working long hours, feeling stressed, or struggling to keep up with your workload, hiring help becomes essential. Long-term stress and exhaustion can lead to

CHAPTER 8: HIRING AND TRAINING STAFF

decreased productivity, poor decision-making, and health issues, which can ultimately affect the overall health of your business. Hiring employees who can share the workload and bring in new perspectives can not only reduce stress but also inject fresh energy into the business.

Lastly, consider hiring help when you want to expand your skillset or improve specific areas of your service. If you feel that certain aspects of your business, like marketing, customer service, or specialized care, are being neglected, bringing in someone with expertise in those areas can elevate your operations. Hiring help is an investment in both your business and your well-being. By recognizing when it's time to bring in additional staff, you can maintain a high standard of service, prevent burnout, and ensure that your business continues to grow and thrive.

Signs You Need Help:
  - Increased Demand: You're consistently fully booked or turning away clients.
  - Decline in Service Quality: Tasks like cleaning, updates, or personalized care are being overlooked.
  - Long Working Hours: You or your current team are stretched too thin.

Types of Roles to Consider:
  - Pet Care Assistants: Handle feeding, cleaning, and exercising pets.
  - Groomers or Trainers: Offer specialized services to expand your offerings.
  - Administrative Staff: Manage bookings, client communication, and records.

Planning for Growth:
  - Start with part-time or seasonal staff during busy periods.
  - Hire based on clear job descriptions to attract candidates with relevant skills and experience.

Training for Quality Pet Care

Comprehensive training is essential for ensuring that your staff is prepared to deliver the high level of care that your clients expect. In the pet care industry, trust is a major factor, and clients need to know that their pets are in safe hands. Well-trained staff not only perform tasks efficiently but also understand the unique needs of each pet, ensuring that animals receive personalized and professional attention. This commitment to quality care can make all the difference in building a strong reputation for your business.

The first step in providing comprehensive training is to create a clear and structured training program that covers all aspects of pet care. Staff should be well-versed in the basics of pet health, behavior, and safety. This includes understanding signs of common illnesses, recognizing behavioral issues, and knowing how to handle different types of pets safely. Whether it's knowing how to safely bathe a dog, manage aggressive behavior, or administer basic first aid, these skills are crucial for maintaining the well-being of the animals in your care.

Another important aspect of training is ensuring that staff understand the importance of communication, both with pets and clients. Staff should be trained to read pets' body language and understand how to approach and care for animals based on their temperaments. This is particularly important for pets that may be nervous, anxious, or reactive. On the client side, communication skills are equally important, as pet owners will want regular updates about their pets' well-being and any issues that may arise. Staff who are well-trained in customer service will foster positive relationships with clients and help build trust.

CHAPTER 8: HIRING AND TRAINING STAFF

Hands-on experience is also key to effective training. Theoretical knowledge is important, but learning through real-world practice allows staff to build confidence in their abilities and better understand how to apply their training. This could include shadowing experienced staff, working directly with pets under supervision, or having a mentor to guide them through difficult situations. Regular assessments and feedback are also valuable, helping staff identify areas where they may need improvement and giving them an opportunity to grow in their roles.

Finally, training should be an ongoing process. As new techniques, tools, or pet care practices emerge, it's important to keep staff updated with the latest information. Continuing education helps staff stay current and ensures that your business maintains the highest standards of care. Whether it's attending workshops, watching training videos, or participating in industry conferences, continuous learning is key to keeping your staff prepared for any situation and ensuring that your pet care business continues to thrive. By investing in comprehensive training, you're not only ensuring the safety and happiness of the pets you care for, but you're also creating a knowledgeable, confident, and professional team that will keep clients coming back.

Core Training Areas:
   - Animal Handling: Teach proper techniques for interacting with different breeds and temperaments.
   - Health and Safety: Train staff to recognize signs of illness, administer medications, and respond to emergencies.
   - Facility Maintenance: Emphasize cleanliness and organization, including safe handling of cleaning supplies.
   - Customer Interaction: Guide staff on professional communication and addressing client concerns.

Onboarding New Employees:
   - Develop a detailed training manual covering your policies, procedures, and expectations.

- Pair new hires with experienced staff for hands-on learning during their initial weeks.
   - Schedule regular check-ins to assess progress and address questions.

Ongoing Training:
   - Hold monthly or quarterly workshops on topics like pet first aid, new care techniques, or customer service skills.
   - Encourage staff to attend industry conferences or online courses, reimbursing costs when possible.

—-

Creating a Positive Work Environment

A positive work environment is essential for fostering employee morale, increasing productivity, and reducing turnover. In any business, but especially in the pet care industry, employees who feel supported, appreciated, and motivated are more likely to perform well, stay with the company long-term, and provide the level of service that clients expect. Creating an environment where employees feel engaged and valued not only enhances their job satisfaction but also contributes to a healthier, more efficient workplace.

One of the key factors in creating a positive work environment is clear and open communication. Employees should feel comfortable expressing their ideas, asking questions, and discussing concerns without fear of judgment. When management listens to employees and actively encourages feedback, it helps build trust and fosters a sense of collaboration. Regular team meetings, one-on-one check-ins, or even informal gatherings can provide employees with a space to voice their opinions and feel heard. This type of communication makes employees feel valued and shows that their input matters.

Recognition and appreciation also play a big role in creating a positive work culture. Simple gestures like thanking staff for their hard work, recognizing their achievements, or celebrating milestones can go a long way in boosting morale. Employees who feel appreciated are more likely to be motivated and take pride in their work. Consider implementing formal recognition programs, such as Employee of the Month awards or regular shout-outs in meetings, to highlight their contributions. Offering small rewards, such as gift cards, extra time off, or team lunches, can also make employees feel valued and help keep the workplace atmosphere positive.

Providing opportunities for growth and development is another crucial element. Employees who feel like they have room to grow within the company are more likely to stay engaged and committed. Offering training programs, promotions, or skill-building opportunities helps employees develop professionally and encourages long-term loyalty. When people know that their hard work can lead to career advancement, they are more invested in their roles and more likely to go the extra mile. Creating a clear path for growth not only benefits employees but also contributes to the overall success of the business.

Finally, fostering a supportive and inclusive work culture is essential for employee well-being. Encouraging teamwork, mutual respect, and a sense of belonging helps create a more enjoyable and collaborative work environment. Pet care can be a physically demanding job, so offering emotional support, flexibility, and a good work-life balance is critical for keeping employees happy and healthy. Encouraging employees to take breaks, ensuring manageable workloads, and promoting a culture of kindness and support can help prevent burnout and maintain high levels of morale. When employees feel supported both professionally and personally, they're more likely to stick around, providing long-term benefits for your business.

By creating a positive work environment, you not only boost employee morale and reduce turnover but also enhance the overall atmosphere of your business. Happy, engaged employees are more likely to provide top-notch care for the pets in your charge and build lasting relationships with clients, contributing to the long-term success and growth of your business.

Key Strategies:
- Open Communication: Foster a culture where staff feel comfortable sharing ideas, concerns, or feedback.
- Recognition and Rewards: Acknowledge hard work with praise, bonuses, or perks like extra time off.
- Team Building: Organize activities such as group outings or team lunches to strengthen camaraderie.
- Clear Expectations: Provide clear guidelines for roles, responsibilities, and performance standards to avoid misunderstandings.

Supportive Policies:
- Offer flexible scheduling, especially during busy periods, to accommodate personal needs.
- Provide resources for stress management, as working with animals can be both rewarding and demanding.

Encouraging Growth:
- Promote from within whenever possible to reward dedication and retain talent.
- Create pathways for career advancement, such as opportunities to specialize in grooming, training, or management roles.

—-

CHAPTER 8: HIRING AND TRAINING STAFF

Key Takeaways

- Hiring additional staff ensures your business can handle growth without sacrificing quality.

    - Comprehensive training equips employees to provide excellent pet care and service.

    - A positive work environment fosters loyalty, teamwork, and overall job satisfaction.

By hiring thoughtfully, investing in training, and cultivating a supportive culture, you'll build a team that shares your vision for exceptional pet care and client satisfaction.

CHAPTER 9: SCALING YOUR BUSINESS

Once my pet care business is up and running, and I've found the right balance between providing excellent care and maintaining smooth daily operations, the next step is clear—scaling. Growing my business allows me to reach more clients, offer a broader range of services, and potentially expand to new locations. However, scaling isn't just about increasing profits—it's about carefully managing growth in a way that maintains the high standards of service my clients expect. In this chapter, I'll explore how to expand my offerings, strategically add new locations, and foster long-term client relationships that keep my business growing for years to come.

One of the most exciting ways to scale a pet care business is by expanding the services I offer. As my reputation grows, I'll have the opportunity to introduce new services that meet the evolving needs of my clients. This could mean adding grooming, pet training, or even specialty services like pet massage or behavioral therapy. I'll discuss how to identify the right services to add based on client demand and market trends, ensuring that these new offerings align with my brand and values. Expanding my services gives me the chance to enhance the customer experience and strengthen my relationship with clients by providing a more comprehensive suite of care options for their pets.

CHAPTER 9: SCALING YOUR BUSINESS

Another key strategy for scaling my pet care business is expanding to new locations. While opening a new location can significantly increase my reach and revenue, it also comes with unique challenges. In this chapter, I'll explore how to approach the decision of when and where to expand, what factors to consider in selecting a new location, and how to ensure the operational consistency between multiple facilities. I'll also discuss how to replicate the success of my initial location while adapting to the needs of each new community. Expanding strategically will allow me to grow my brand and service area without compromising the quality of care or customer satisfaction that my business is known for.

Scaling my business also means strengthening the relationships I have with my existing clients. Retaining loyal customers is crucial to sustaining long-term growth, and fostering these relationships will ensure that I continue to thrive in a competitive market. In this chapter, I'll discuss how to keep my clients engaged and satisfied as my business grows. Whether it's through personalized care, loyalty programs, or regular check-ins, I'll explore strategies for building stronger connections with clients and encouraging repeat business. Loyal clients not only continue to use my services but also refer new customers, helping to fuel my business growth organically.

Finally, I'll cover how to manage the logistical and operational challenges that come with scaling. As my business grows, I'll face the need for more staff, additional training, and possibly even upgrades to my equipment or facilities. I'll discuss how to manage these changes while keeping my focus on maintaining the same level of care and customer service that allowed me to succeed in the first place. Scaling my pet care business requires careful planning and a clear vision, but with the right strategies in place, it can open doors to even greater success.

In this chapter, I'll lay out a roadmap for scaling my pet care business in a way that is sustainable, strategic, and aligned with my long-term goals. Whether it's expanding services, opening new locations, or deepening relationships with clients, the strategies discussed here will help me grow my business while ensuring I continue to provide the best possible care to the pets I look after. By focusing on thoughtful expansion and maintaining the integrity of my business model, I'll be able to take my pet care business to the next level and secure its place as a trusted name in the community.

—-

Expanding Your Services

Expanding your services is a strategic way to grow your pet care business, attract more clients, and increase revenue. By diversifying your offerings, you can meet a broader range of needs within the pet care community, making your business a one-stop solution for pet owners. This not only boosts customer satisfaction but also strengthens your position in the competitive pet care market. Clients are more likely to stay loyal when they can rely on your business for multiple aspects of their pets' care, reducing their need to search for other service providers.

One way to expand your services is by adding specialized options, such as grooming, training, or boarding, that cater to specific needs. For instance, offering professional grooming services can attract pet owners who are looking for a place where their pets can be bathed, trimmed, and treated by experts. Training services, such as obedience classes or behavioral training, can also be valuable for pet owners who want to address issues like leash pulling or separation anxiety. By providing these additional services, you can not only increase your revenue streams but also build stronger relationships with clients by becoming a go-to resource for all their pet care needs.

Another option for expanding your services is to offer pet wellness or health-related options, such as nutritional counseling, preventive care, or pet

CHAPTER 9: SCALING YOUR BUSINESS

massage therapy. Many pet owners are becoming more conscious of their pets' health and well-being, and offering services that focus on prevention and wellness can help you tap into this growing market. For example, offering advice on the best diets for different breeds, supplements, or even dental care can provide significant value to your clients. By expanding your offerings in this area, you show that you care about the overall health of the pets in your care, which can help build trust and loyalty.

Additionally, creating customizable care packages or membership plans can attract clients who prefer convenience and consistency. For example, offering monthly or quarterly subscription plans that include a combination of grooming, training, and other services can help pet owners manage their pets' care more efficiently. These packages can also offer discounted rates, which make them more attractive to customers. A membership model can build a stable, predictable revenue stream for your business while offering clients a more personalized experience.

Finally, consider offering services that cater to the growing demand for convenience, such as pet transportation, pet sitting, or mobile grooming. These services make it easier for pet owners to care for their pets without leaving their homes or dealing with transportation issues. Offering mobile grooming, for example, allows clients to have their pets groomed at home, which can be particularly convenient for those with busy schedules or pets that are anxious about visiting a grooming facility. Adding such services gives you a competitive edge and can attract new customers who value convenience.

By diversifying your offerings, you create multiple revenue streams, enhance customer satisfaction, and make your business a more comprehensive solution for pet owners. This not only helps attract a wider audience but also increases client retention, as customers will appreciate the convenience of having all their pet care needs met in one place. Expanding your services is a smart way to future-proof your business and establish yourself as a trusted, reliable resource for pet owners.

Steps to Expand Services:
- Research Demand: Survey your clients or analyze market trends to identify high-demand services.
- Start Small: Introduce one new service at a time, such as grooming, training, or pet sitting.
- Invest in Equipment and Staff: Ensure you have the necessary tools, space, and trained personnel to deliver new services effectively.

Examples of Add-On Services:
- Pet Spa Treatments: Offer luxury options like massages or aromatherapy for pets.
- Mobile Services: Provide grooming or veterinary support at clients' homes.
- Pet Boutique: Sell premium pet food, toys, and accessories at your location.

Bundling and Packaging:
- Create packages that combine boarding with additional services, like "Stay & Groom" or "Training Camp."
- Offer loyalty discounts for clients who book multiple services.

—-

Adding New Locations

Opening additional locations is a major milestone for any business, and it requires thoughtful planning and execution to ensure its success. Expanding your pet care business into new areas allows you to reach more clients, increase revenue, and solidify your brand's presence in the market. However,

CHAPTER 9: SCALING YOUR BUSINESS

this expansion must be approached strategically to avoid spreading your resources too thin and to ensure that each new location operates smoothly and effectively.

The first step in adding new locations is conducting thorough market research. It's essential to understand the demand for pet care services in the new area, as well as the level of competition. Look at factors such as local demographics, pet ownership rates, and the presence of other pet care businesses in the area. If you're considering opening in a particular neighborhood or city, assess whether the local community values high-quality pet care services and whether your offerings align with their needs. By researching and identifying a market that has a demand for your services, you can reduce the risk of failure and ensure that your new location will attract customers.

Once you've identified a suitable location, securing the right staff is crucial. Hiring experienced employees who share your company's values and commitment to high-quality pet care will be key to maintaining consistency across locations. Consider the training and development needs for your new team members, and ensure they are well-prepared to deliver the same level of care and customer service that your original location is known for. It's also important to maintain strong leadership at each new location, whether through local managers or supervisors who understand the culture of your business and can ensure that operations run smoothly.

The logistics of running multiple locations also require a strong organizational structure. Consider using technology to streamline operations, from scheduling and booking systems to inventory management and communication platforms. Centralizing important tasks, such as financial tracking or customer data management, can help ensure that everything runs cohesively across locations. Clear processes and procedures should be in place to help with training, quality control, and maintaining standards, so that each location offers the same high level of service. Regular communication between locations is vital to ensure that best practices are shared and that all locations are working toward the same goals.

Marketing plays a key role in the success of a new location. When opening an additional branch, it's important to market it both to your existing customers and to the local community. Utilize your established reputation to attract clients from your original location to the new one, offering promotions, discounts, or loyalty rewards for those who use services at both locations. Local advertising methods, such as flyers, social media targeted at the new area, or partnerships with other local businesses, can help raise awareness in the new market. Hosting grand opening events or community-focused initiatives can also attract attention and drive traffic to your new location.

Lastly, opening additional locations requires adequate financial planning. You need to ensure that the costs of expansion—such as leasing new space, renovating, staffing, and marketing—are covered, and that your business can handle the additional operational costs. Creating a solid financial plan that accounts for both the initial investment and the expected returns is essential. Having a clear budget and timeline for profitability will help you stay on track and make informed decisions during the expansion process.

In summary, adding new locations is an exciting growth opportunity for your business but requires detailed planning and careful execution. By conducting thorough market research, building a strong team, implementing streamlined processes, marketing effectively, and managing finances carefully, you can set your business up for long-term success and create a consistent, high-quality experience for customers at each location. Expanding strategically ensures that your business remains strong and sustainable as it grows.

How to Prepare:
   - Evaluate Demand: Identify neighborhoods or cities with a high concentration of pet owners and limited competition.
   - Standardize Operations: Develop clear protocols for all aspects of your

business, from pet care to customer service, to ensure consistency across locations.
  - Secure Funding: Assess your financial readiness and explore funding options, such as business loans or investors.

Managing Multiple Locations:
  - Consider franchising to expand your brand while leveraging local entrepreneurs.
  - Use management software to monitor operations and finances across locations in real time.
  - Appoint experienced managers to oversee daily operations at each site.

Potential Challenges:
  - Maintaining quality control as your business grows.
  - Navigating local zoning and licensing regulations for new areas.
  - Balancing the demands of overseeing multiple locations.

—-

Building Long-Term Client Relationships

Building long-term client relationships is crucial to the sustained success of any business, including those in the pet care industry. While attracting new customers is important for growth, retaining loyal clients is often more cost-effective and beneficial in the long run. Loyal customers not only provide a steady stream of revenue but also act as ambassadors for your brand, recommending your services to others and helping you build a solid reputation. Fostering lasting relationships with clients requires a focus on trust, communication, and consistently delivering exceptional service.

One of the key ways to build long-term client relationships is through excellent customer service. When clients feel valued and heard, they are more likely to return and continue using your services. This means going beyond the basics of delivering the service they paid for and truly connecting with them on a personal level. Taking the time to learn about their pets, their preferences, and their specific needs helps create a bond of trust and shows that you care. Personalized interactions, such as remembering a client's pet's birthday or following up after an appointment, go a long way in building a strong, loyal relationship.

Consistency is also essential when it comes to client retention. Clients need to feel that they can rely on your business to meet their needs every time they visit. This means maintaining high standards of care, ensuring that your staff is well-trained and professional, and addressing any concerns or issues promptly. By consistently delivering quality service, you create a sense of reliability that clients can count on, which encourages them to stay with your business long-term.

Another important factor is communication. Keeping clients informed about their pets' care and progress helps build transparency and trust. Regular updates, whether through phone calls, emails, or text messages, allow clients to feel involved and reassured about the care their pets are receiving. It's also important to listen to feedback from clients, both positive and negative, and make improvements when necessary. When clients see that their opinions are valued and acted upon, they are more likely to continue their relationship with your business.

Lastly, offering loyalty programs or incentives is a great way to encourage repeat business and show appreciation to your most loyal clients. Discounts, referral bonuses, or exclusive offers for returning customers can help keep clients engaged and motivated to continue using your services. A well-designed loyalty program can reward clients for their continued business while also providing them with tangible benefits.

CHAPTER 9: SCALING YOUR BUSINESS

In conclusion, building long-term client relationships is a strategic investment that pays off in the form of customer retention, positive word-of-mouth, and consistent revenue. By focusing on exceptional customer service, consistency, communication, and incentives, you can foster strong, lasting relationships with your clients. In turn, these loyal customers will not only continue to support your business but also help you grow through their ongoing trust and recommendations.

Strategies for Retention:
  - Personalized Communication: Use email or text updates to celebrate milestones, such as a pet's birthday or anniversary with your business.
  - Loyalty Programs: Reward repeat clients with discounts, free services, or exclusive perks.
  - Solicit Feedback: Regularly ask for client input on your services and act on their suggestions to show you value their opinions.

Community Engagement:
  - Host events like pet adoption days, open houses, or workshops on pet care.
  - Sponsor local pet-related events or charities to boost your visibility and goodwill.

Exceptional Customer Service:
  - Provide consistent updates on their pets during boarding or other services.
  - Address any concerns promptly and professionally to build trust and confidence.

The Power of Referrals:
  - Encourage satisfied clients to refer friends and family. Offer referral bonuses, such as discounts for both the referrer and the new client.
  - Collaborate with veterinarians, pet stores, and other local businesses to gain more referrals.

Key Takeaways

- Expanding your services allows you to meet more client needs while increasing revenue streams.

- Adding new locations can grow your brand, but careful planning and standardization are essential.

- Long-term client relationships are the backbone of your business; invest in loyalty and community engagement to ensure continued success.

Scaling your pet care business requires strategic thinking, adaptability, and a commitment to maintaining the quality that earned your initial success. With a solid plan, you can grow sustainably while continuing to delight pets and their owners.

CHAPTER 10: REAL-LIFE TESTIMONIES FROM SUCCESSFUL DOG BOARDING OWNERS

Starting a dog boarding business can feel overwhelming, especially when faced with the complexities of running a service-oriented company. One of the best ways to gain valuable insights and avoid common pitfalls is by learning from those who've already walked the path. In this chapter, I'll highlight real-life stories from seasoned dog boarding business owners, offering a behind-the-scenes look at their journeys, successes, and the lessons they've learned along the way. These firsthand accounts provide not only inspiration but also practical advice for newcomers who are looking to navigate the challenges and opportunities of this rewarding industry.

Hearing directly from experienced entrepreneurs gives me the chance to understand the realities of building a dog boarding business. These stories often start with humble beginnings, where passion for animals led to the first steps of offering services from home or a small facility. From there, many of these owners faced growing pains, such as managing unexpected expenses, navigating the complexities of staffing, or learning how to stand out in a competitive market. Through trial and error, they gained the knowledge that now guides their successful operations. I'll share these stories in this chapter to show that success doesn't happen overnight, but with perseverance and dedication, it's certainly attainable.

One of the key takeaways from these experienced business owners is how they turned challenges into opportunities. Whether it was learning the hard way about the importance of setting clear policies, managing customer expectations, or addressing staff turnover, many entrepreneurs found that their biggest mistakes ultimately led to growth. Their stories are full of lessons on how to handle adversity, adapt to changing market conditions, and stay focused on what matters most: providing excellent care for the dogs and building trust with their clients. I'll dive into these lessons, offering a blueprint for beginners to follow, so they can avoid common mistakes and set themselves up for success from the start.

In addition to learning from mistakes, hearing about the strategies that have led to success is equally valuable. Many successful dog boarding business owners have shared how they were able to build a loyal customer base, scale their operations, and establish themselves as trusted names in their communities. From leveraging word-of-mouth referrals and social media marketing to offering unique services that set them apart, these entrepreneurs have developed strategies that have allowed them to thrive in a competitive industry. In this chapter, I'll highlight these strategies and explain how newcomers can implement them in their own businesses to achieve similar success.

Finally, this chapter will offer practical advice on how to take the first steps in starting a dog boarding business, from finding the right location and obtaining necessary licenses to creating a solid business plan and setting competitive pricing. The seasoned business owners featured in this chapter will offer a wealth of actionable tips that can help beginners avoid common pitfalls and hit the ground running. With their insights and advice, aspiring entrepreneurs will gain the confidence they need to navigate the challenges ahead and build a successful dog boarding business.

Through these stories and lessons, I hope to inspire new dog boarding business owners to learn from the experiences of others while also encouraging them to trust their instincts and passion for pets. This chapter provides a comprehensive look at the journey of building a business from the ground up, helping newcomers feel more prepared and confident as they embark on their own entrepreneurial adventure. By following the advice of those who have already been through the ups and downs, I can set myself up for long-term success in the dog boarding industry.

—-

1. Inspiring Stories of Startups

Story 1: From Backyard Hobby to Thriving Business

Jennifer's love for dogs began as a simple desire to help out friends and family. When she saw that they needed a reliable person to care for their pets while they were away, she didn't hesitate to offer her backyard as a safe space. At first, it was just a small arrangement—watching one or two dogs at a time, offering them food, exercise, and the attention they needed. She enjoyed every moment of it, finding joy in seeing the dogs happy and well-cared for. What started as a favor to those closest to her slowly began to grow into something much more.

As the word spread, more people started asking if Jennifer could watch their dogs while they were away. The simple service she offered became highly in demand, and soon, friends of friends were reaching out. Jennifer saw an opportunity to turn her passion into something bigger. What had been a backyard hobby was beginning to feel like a potential business. After a lot of thought, she made the decision to fully commit to this new path, knowing that it was the right move for her.

She invested in creating a proper facility, one that could accommodate more dogs and provide a range of services. It wasn't just about watching the dogs anymore; Jennifer wanted to create an environment where pets could feel safe, loved, and entertained. She expanded her offerings to include grooming and training, both of which were welcomed by the community. As the business grew, she added staff to help meet the increasing demand, carefully selecting people who shared her deep love and respect for animals.

As her pet care business continued to thrive, Jennifer found that her focus was no longer just about caring for dogs—it was about creating a trusted place where pet owners could feel secure in leaving their furry friends. The word-of-mouth referrals kept coming in, each new customer bringing with them new pets and, often, new challenges. But Jennifer was prepared. She had built a strong foundation, one that allowed her to provide the highest level of care while balancing the day-to-day logistics of a growing business.

Today, Jennifer's business is a far cry from the small backyard operation it once was. With the capacity to care for up to 30 dogs, she has established herself as a trusted name in the community. What started as a small, side project for a dog lover has blossomed into a thriving business, one that not only supports her but also provides jobs for others who share her passion. Looking back, Jennifer never could have imagined how far her simple idea would take her, but she's grateful every day for the journey that turned a hobby into a life-changing endeavor.

- Key Takeaway: Start small but think big. Focus on quality care, and your reputation will grow naturally.

Story 2: Turning Passion into a Franchise

Michael and Laura's journey began in their small rural community, where they saw a gap in the market for quality pet care. They decided to start a dog boarding service that would focus on providing a safe and comfortable environment for pets while their owners were away. From the beginning, they made it their top priority to offer personalized attention to each dog, treating them as if they were their own. They quickly built a loyal customer base, thanks to their dedication to providing excellent care and creating a welcoming atmosphere.

At first, the business was small, but their commitment to customer service and consistent quality quickly paid off. Word spread, and more and more pet owners began trusting Michael and Laura with their dogs. They found that by focusing on building strong relationships with clients and ensuring every pet received individualized care, they could stand out from other services in the area. Their clients appreciated the attention to detail and the peace of mind knowing their pets were well-cared for, and the positive reviews and referrals began to pour in.

As demand grew, Michael and Laura knew they had to expand their operations. Instead of settling for just one location, they made the decision to scale their business. They carefully researched new areas where they could offer the same level of care and customer service. Their first expansion was successful, and they followed up by opening additional locations, each one maintaining the same high standards of care that had made the first location such a success. They were meticulous in their hiring process, ensuring that each new team member shared their passion for animals and their commitment to excellent service.

Over the next six years, their business continued to grow. They had transformed from a single dog boarding location into a network of five thriving facilities. Michael and Laura worked tirelessly to maintain their business's reputation, focusing on consistent service and a personal touch that made them stand out. They also took steps to ensure that each new location was equipped with the same level of care and comfort that had made the original one so popular.

Looking back on their journey, Michael and Laura are proud of how far they've come. Their dedication to excellent customer service and maintaining high standards has not only helped them grow their business but also established them as a trusted name in the pet care industry. While their company is now much larger than when they started, they continue to prioritize the same core values that allowed them to succeed in the first place. Their commitment to their customers and their pets remains as strong as ever.

- Key Takeaway: Standardizing operations is crucial for scaling while preserving quality.

Story 3: Innovating for Niche Clients

Ravi, a savvy entrepreneur with a keen eye for opportunity, noticed a gap in the urban market for luxury pet care services. While there were plenty of dog boarding facilities available, most of them offered standard, no-frills accommodations. Ravi, however, saw potential in catering to a niche market—high-income pet owners who wanted more than just basic care for their dogs. He knew that these clients valued their pets like family members and were willing to pay a premium for top-notch services. With this insight, he set out to create a luxury dog boarding experience unlike anything available in the area.

To make his vision a reality, Ravi spared no expense in designing his facility. Each dog would have its own private suite, offering a level of comfort and privacy far beyond the usual kennel setup. The rooms were equipped with plush bedding, soothing music, and climate control, ensuring that each pet felt at home. On top of that, Ravi introduced gourmet meals prepared with high-quality ingredients, tailored to meet the specific dietary needs of each dog. This attention to detail was something that set his business apart from

CHAPTER 10: REAL-LIFE TESTIMONIES FROM SUCCESSFUL DOG...

the rest—he wasn't just offering a place to sleep, but a luxury experience for pets.

One of the most innovative features of Ravi's facility was the on-demand video monitoring system, which allowed pet owners to check in on their dogs at any time via a secure app. This feature quickly became a hit with clients, as it gave them peace of mind knowing they could see their pets whenever they wished. The ability to check in on their dogs made the experience feel more personal and reassuring, especially for owners who had never left their pets in someone else's care before.

Ravi's unique approach to dog boarding attracted a growing number of high-income clients who were looking for more than just a place to leave their dogs while they were away. His reputation quickly spread throughout the community, and his facility became a local sensation. Word of mouth, combined with strategic marketing, led to a steady stream of new clients. Pet owners appreciated the level of care and luxury their dogs received, and they were more than happy to pay a premium for the exceptional service.

Within a short period, Ravi had successfully established his luxury dog boarding business as the go-to option for pet owners in the area. His focus on creating a high-end experience for both pets and their owners allowed him to carve out a niche in the competitive pet care market. By combining innovation, luxury, and top-tier service, Ravi not only met a market need but also created a brand that resonated deeply with his target audience, solidifying his place as a leader in the pet care industry.

- Key Takeaway: Identify a niche and tailor your services to meet unique client needs.

—-

2. Lessons Learned from Mistakes and Successes

Lesson 1: The Importance of Planning

Many entrepreneurs, especially those just starting out, often admit that they underestimated the startup costs involved in launching a new business. While they had a clear vision for their product or service, the reality of managing expenses quickly set in. The costs of securing a location, purchasing equipment, hiring employees, and covering other initial expenses can add up much faster than anticipated. It's easy to overlook these financial demands when excitement and passion for the business are high, but this oversight can lead to early struggles and financial strain.

In the early days, many business owners find themselves scrambling to cover these unexpected costs, leading to cash flow issues. If the money isn't flowing in as quickly as expected, it can create a snowball effect—delayed payments, missed opportunities, and increased stress. Without proper financial planning, business owners might find themselves in a tough position, unable to cover their bills or even pay employees on time. These financial struggles can cause significant anxiety and potentially derail the success of the business before it even has a chance to grow.

To prevent these issues, it's essential for entrepreneurs to dedicate time and attention to budgeting and financial planning before opening their doors. A solid financial plan should account for both anticipated and unforeseen expenses, including an emergency fund to cover unexpected costs. Having a clear understanding of how much capital is required to keep the business running in its early stages can help avoid the pitfalls of underestimating expenses. It also ensures that there's enough cash flow to cover daily operations, even if profits take time to materialize.

Additionally, business owners can benefit from seeking expert advice when it comes to financial planning. This could mean consulting with accountants or financial advisors who can help create realistic financial projections and ensure the business is prepared for the challenges that come with managing finances. These professionals can also provide valuable insights into areas where expenses can be reduced or optimized, helping to create a more sustainable financial structure.

By prioritizing financial planning and budgeting, business owners can avoid many of the common mistakes that lead to cash flow problems. A well-thought-out budget, paired with careful attention to cash management, can make all the difference in the early stages of a business. It provides the foundation necessary for growth and allows entrepreneurs to focus on their long-term goals, knowing that their financial position is secure and manageable.

- Mistake Example: One common mistake that many business owners make is expanding too quickly without a clear financial strategy in place. This was the case for one particular owner who saw early success and assumed that rapid growth was the key to furthering the business. Eager to meet increasing demand, they opened additional locations and hired more staff, believing that the expansion would naturally lead to more profits. However, the excitement of growth clouded their judgment when it came to financial planning.

Without a solid financial strategy, the owner quickly ran into cash flow problems. The costs associated with running multiple locations—such as rent, payroll, and inventory—far outpaced the business's revenue. The increased operational expenses were not properly anticipated, and there was no financial cushion in place to support the expansion. As a result, the business was unable to meet its financial obligations, and after only a short period of time, the owner was forced to temporarily close some of the new locations to stay afloat.

This situation could have been avoided with more careful planning. Had the owner taken the time to assess the long-term financial impact of expansion—factoring in everything from operating costs to the time needed for new locations to become profitable—they might have realized that they were stretching their resources too thin. Expanding a business requires careful consideration of both short-term cash flow and long-term financial health. With a more strategic approach, the owner could have grown at a steadier pace, ensuring that the business remained financially stable and sustainable.

This mistake serves as a reminder that expansion should be driven by both demand and careful financial planning. Quick growth can seem appealing, but without a strong financial foundation, it can quickly turn into a major setback. Business owners should make sure they have the resources in place to support growth and should prioritize building a sustainable financial strategy that allows for scalability without risking their core operations.

Lesson 2: Value Your Staff

Hiring the right people is one of the most important decisions a business owner can make, especially when it comes to industries like pet care, where the quality of service is so closely tied to the skills and attitudes of the staff. When you hire employees who are not only capable but also passionate about what they do, they're more likely to provide excellent care and create a positive experience for customers. On the other hand, if employees aren't a good fit or haven't been properly trained, it can result in mistakes, misunderstandings, and an overall decline in the quality of service. This is why investing in the right people and their ongoing training is essential to any business's success.

Training isn't just about teaching employees how to perform specific tasks—it's about instilling company values, ensuring consistency, and fostering a sense of ownership and pride in their work. When staff are well-trained, they feel more confident in their roles and are better equipped to handle challenges. Whether it's learning the specific needs of different pets or understanding how to communicate with clients, training helps employees meet expectations and exceed them. This leads to higher customer satisfaction, as clients are more likely to return and recommend the service when they see that their pets are in good hands.

However, neglecting the needs of your staff, whether it's by skipping proper training or failing to provide the right support, can have significant consequences. Employees who feel underprepared or undervalued are more likely to leave, leading to high turnover rates. Constantly hiring and training new staff can become time-consuming and costly, not to mention disruptive to the business. It also creates an environment where customers may experience inconsistent service, as new employees may not be fully up to speed with the business's standards or culture.

The key to retaining good staff and ensuring high-quality service is to prioritize their needs and invest in their growth. Offering ongoing training, creating opportunities for advancement, and fostering a positive work environment can help employees feel motivated and appreciated. When employees feel like they're part of something larger, they're more likely to stay and contribute positively to the business. This not only reduces turnover but also helps to build a more reliable and skilled team.

In the end, the investment in staff training and development pays off. A knowledgeable and motivated team will provide better service, improve customer satisfaction, and help the business grow. By making staff development a priority, you create a stable foundation for your business, where both employees and customers thrive.

- Success Example: A boarding facility owner once shared how offering competitive wages and prioritizing professional development transformed their business. In the early days, the owner faced challenges with high employee turnover and the constant need to hire new staff. The service quality was inconsistent, which negatively impacted customer satisfaction. Realizing that the root of the problem was employee dissatisfaction, the owner decided to make a change. Instead of just focusing on the business's bottom line, they chose to invest in their staff.

The owner began by offering competitive wages that were higher than what other local businesses paid for similar positions. This helped attract more experienced and motivated candidates, ensuring the team was made up of individuals who truly cared about providing excellent pet care. But the commitment didn't stop at wages. The owner also introduced professional development programs, providing staff with the tools and knowledge they needed to advance in their roles. From learning more about animal behavior to improving customer service skills, the investment in training made employees feel valued and empowered.

The results were immediate. Staff retention improved significantly, as employees felt more appreciated and saw a clear path for career growth. With a stable team in place, the quality of care for the pets also improved. The team worked more efficiently, and their passion for the job was evident in how they treated the animals and interacted with the clients. Pet owners began to notice the difference and returned to the facility with greater confidence, knowing that their pets were being cared for by a dedicated, experienced team.

As the business grew, the owner found that the positive work culture they had created became a driving force behind the success of their facility. Employees were not just doing their job—they were motivated to go above and beyond because they felt valued. This loyalty and motivation led to exceptional customer service and an overall improvement in the business's reputation. Word of mouth spread, and the business saw a steady increase in clients.

In the end, by offering competitive wages and investing in professional development, the boarding facility owner created a loyal, skilled, and motivated team that was crucial to the success and growth of the business. This approach proved that taking care of your employees not only benefits them but also benefits the business as a whole.

Lesson 3: Listen to Customers

Ignoring customer feedback can be a costly mistake for any business. While it might be tempting to stick to the way things are done or assume that customers are satisfied without asking, neglecting their input can lead to lost opportunities and, ultimately, lost business. Many successful business owners have credited their growth to the fact that they actively listen to their customers and make changes based on their feedback. Customers often offer valuable insights into what works well and what needs improvement, and by acting on these suggestions, businesses can better meet their clients' needs and build stronger relationships.

One example is a dog boarding facility that received consistent feedback from clients about the challenges of getting their pets dropped off during regular hours. Many customers worked long hours or had unpredictable schedules, making it difficult to arrive within the set drop-off window. Instead of ignoring the issue, the owner decided to extend the facility's drop-off hours to accommodate these clients. This small change made a big difference, as it allowed more people to use the service and improved overall customer satisfaction. Clients appreciated that their needs were being heard, and many returned to the facility for future bookings.

Another common example of acting on customer feedback comes from business owners who introduce new services based on what their clients want. For instance, a pet care facility that initially only offered boarding might have clients request additional services like grooming, training, or even daycare options. By listening to those suggestions, the owner could expand the range of services offered, which not only generated more revenue but also kept clients coming back for a one-stop shop for all their pet care needs. Offering services that customers are asking for can significantly enhance a business's appeal, turning a basic service into something more comprehensive and valuable.

Some owners also find success by using feedback to improve the customer experience. A few might receive complaints about the cleanliness or comfort of the facilities, prompting them to invest in better amenities or enhance their cleaning protocols. While this type of feedback may seem critical at first, taking it seriously and using it as an opportunity to improve can lead to better customer retention and a stronger reputation.

Overall, business owners who regularly gather, listen to, and act on customer feedback tend to build stronger businesses. Whether it's adjusting hours, expanding services, or improving the overall experience, taking customer suggestions seriously can create a loyal customer base and fuel growth. When clients see that their opinions matter and lead to positive changes, they are more likely to feel valued and continue doing business with you.

- Mistake Example: One entrepreneur learned a valuable lesson about the importance of addressing customer concerns when they lost several clients after dismissing complaints about cleanliness. At first, the business owner didn't take the feedback seriously, assuming the complaints were minor or overly critical. They believed that their staff was doing a good job and didn't see the need for any changes. However, as more customers voiced similar concerns, the business owner's refusal to act on the feedback led to a noticeable decline in customer satisfaction.

The issue was particularly important in the pet care industry, where cleanliness and hygiene are a top priority for clients. Pet owners trust that the facility where they leave their animals will be clean, safe, and comfortable. When customers started noticing a lack of attention to cleanliness, they began to lose confidence in the business, and some of them stopped coming back altogether. Word spread quickly, and the reputation of the business took a hit.

Had the entrepreneur addressed the complaints promptly, they might have been able to resolve the issue before it became a major problem. Instead of brushing off the concerns, they could have implemented a better cleaning routine, brought in additional staff if needed, or upgraded certain areas of the facility to ensure it met the high standards clients expected. By taking immediate action, the owner could have not only retained existing customers but also enhanced their reputation as a business that values client feedback.

This experience highlights the importance of being receptive to customer feedback and acting on it in a timely manner. Ignoring or dismissing concerns can lead to frustration, decreased loyalty, and lost business. Customers are more likely to stay loyal to a business that listens to their concerns and works to improve. In the long run, addressing complaints promptly can help build stronger relationships with clients and keep a business on the path to success.

—-

3. Advice for Beginners

Start with Passion but Build with Strategy

Many successful business owners in the pet care industry have shared that while passion for animals is essential, it must be paired with a strong business plan to ensure long-term success. Starting a business based on love for animals is a great motivator, and it helps owners stay connected to the core mission of providing high-quality care. However, passion alone is not enough to navigate the complexities of running a business, from managing finances to scaling operations and handling customer service. Without a solid strategy, even the most enthusiastic pet lover may struggle to keep the business afloat.

A strong business plan allows owners to turn their passion into a viable, sustainable enterprise. It helps define the vision, set clear goals, and map out the steps necessary to achieve them. For example, a well-structured plan will include detailed financial projections, a clear pricing strategy, marketing plans, and a roadmap for future growth. Without these elements in place, a business is at risk of running into cash flow issues, overextending itself, or losing focus on what matters most to clients.

One key aspect of building a business strategy is understanding the market and competition. Owners must assess the local demand for their services, determine their target audience, and set competitive prices. They also need to evaluate their strengths and weaknesses, ensuring they're offering something unique that stands out in a crowded market. By taking a strategic approach, owners can position their business for success, not just by being passionate, but by addressing real customer needs in a way that resonates with the community.

Another important part of building with strategy is planning for the future. A solid business plan includes steps for growth and scalability, such as expanding to multiple locations, offering additional services, or hiring new staff. It also involves setting up systems for managing daily operations efficiently. As the business grows, it becomes increasingly difficult to maintain the level of care and service that customers expect without proper systems and processes in place.

Ultimately, successful pet care business owners understand that passion for animals is a powerful driving force, but it must be supported by careful planning, strategy, and organization. A well-executed business plan not only helps owners stay on track but also ensures that their love for animals translates into a thriving and sustainable business. By combining passion with strategy, owners can build a business that serves both their clients and their long-term goals.

- Tip: Research your market thoroughly, including local competition and client demographics.

Don't Skimp on Quality

Whether it's the facility, staff, or equipment, investing in quality upfront pays off in client trust and satisfaction.
   - Tip: Keep facilities clean, well-maintained, and welcoming for pets and their owners.

Stay Adaptable

The pet care industry is constantly evolving, with new trends, technologies, and customer preferences emerging regularly. Successful business owners in this field understand that staying adaptable is key to long-term success. By being willing to evolve and respond to changes in the market, owners can not only meet the current needs of their clients but also stay ahead of the competition. One example of adaptability is the growing demand for eco-friendly options. As consumers become more environmentally conscious, pet owners are increasingly seeking sustainable pet care products and services, such as eco-friendly grooming products, biodegradable waste bags, and green building materials for pet facilities. Businesses that embrace these trends can attract a new customer base that prioritizes sustainability.

In addition to environmental trends, pet care needs are becoming more diverse. Many clients now look for specialized services that cater to the specific needs of their pets, such as tailored diets, senior pet care, or services for pets with disabilities. The most successful pet care businesses are those that take the time to understand the unique requirements of their clients and adapt their services to meet those demands. For example, offering specialized boarding options for elderly pets or creating a more serene environment for anxious animals can help differentiate a business from competitors who offer more generic services.

Another example of adaptability is incorporating technology into the business. Many pet care facilities now offer digital tools such as apps for booking, pet tracking, and communication with owners. By embracing these technologies, businesses can streamline operations and offer a higher level of convenience to clients. It's not just about keeping up with trends; it's about enhancing the customer experience and making it easier for pet owners to interact with the business.

However, staying adaptable doesn't mean constantly chasing every new trend. It's important for owners to evaluate trends carefully and assess whether they align with the business's values and long-term goals. Implementing changes should be a thoughtful process, ensuring that any new offerings or changes are sustainable and truly beneficial to both the business and its clients. For instance, offering eco-friendly products might not make sense for every pet care facility, depending on the local market or the type of services offered.

Ultimately, successful pet care business owners know that staying adaptable requires a balance of innovation, customer awareness, and strategic planning. By listening to clients, keeping an eye on industry trends, and remaining open to change, business owners can ensure their services stay relevant and continue to meet the needs of the ever-evolving pet care landscape.

- Tip: Stay informed through industry publications and attend pet care

CHAPTER 10: REAL-LIFE TESTIMONIES FROM SUCCESSFUL DOG...

conferences to keep your services competitive.

Build a Network

Building a strong network is a crucial strategy for success in the pet care industry. By collaborating with veterinarians, pet stores, and other local businesses, pet care owners can create valuable referral opportunities and enhance their credibility within the community. When businesses work together, they not only expand their reach but also foster a sense of trust and partnership that benefits everyone involved. For example, a veterinarian who trusts a local dog boarding facility may refer clients needing boarding services, knowing their pets will be well cared for. In turn, the pet care business can recommend the veterinarian to clients who need professional medical care for their animals. This reciprocal relationship helps both businesses thrive by sharing clientele and supporting each other's success.

In addition to veterinarians, collaborating with local pet stores offers numerous opportunities for cross-promotion. Pet stores often attract a steady flow of pet owners who may need boarding, grooming, or training services for their animals. By partnering with a local pet store, pet care owners can offer discounts, loyalty programs, or special deals for store customers, encouraging them to try out additional services. The store, in turn, can refer their customers to the pet care business, knowing they're sending them to a trusted service provider. This collaboration not only creates new opportunities but also reinforces the local business community, fostering a sense of support and loyalty.

Networking with other local businesses also opens doors to wider community engagement. For example, partnering with a local coffee shop or fitness center could lead to joint promotions or community events, further boosting visibility and brand recognition. Hosting pet-related events in collaboration with these businesses—such as pet adoption days, pet wellness seminars, or holiday-themed events—can draw in a broader audience and increase foot traffic. These events give business owners the chance to showcase their services while building relationships with other entrepreneurs and potential customers.

Beyond gaining referrals, networking with local businesses also boosts credibility and trust in the community. When customers see that a pet care facility is connected to reputable veterinarians, pet stores, and other trusted local businesses, they are more likely to trust the services offered. Building these connections helps establish the business as a reliable part of the local ecosystem, which can be invaluable when clients are deciding where to place their trust in caring for their pets.

Overall, building a network through collaborations and partnerships with veterinarians, pet stores, and other local businesses not only creates more opportunities for referrals but also strengthens the overall reputation of a pet care business. By supporting each other, businesses can grow together, ultimately benefiting both their clients and the broader community.

- Tip: Join local pet care associations or online communities to build connections and share knowledge.

—-

Key Takeaways

- Stories from successful dog boarding owners illustrate the power of perseverance, innovation, and dedication to quality.
    - Mistakes are valuable learning opportunities; listen to feedback, plan carefully, and value your team.
    - Beginners should focus on pairing their passion with strategy, adapting

to industry trends, and building strong networks.

These real-life experiences and lessons offer practical guidance and encouragement for anyone embarking on their journey in the dog boarding business.

CHAPTER 11: FAQS ABOUT STARTING A DOG BOARDING BUSINESS

Launching a dog boarding business comes with many questions and uncertainties. This chapter addresses common concerns, provides answers to legal, financial, and operational queries, and offers tips for handling challenging situations effectively.

—-

1. Common Concerns from New Business Owners

How do I attract my first clients?
  - Start by advertising locally through flyers, community boards, and social media platforms.
  - Offer discounts for first-time customers or referral bonuses to existing clients.
  - Partner with local veterinarians, pet stores, and groomers to gain referrals.

What if I can't afford a large facility to start?
  - Begin with a smaller, home-based setup if zoning laws permit, and grow gradually.

CHAPTER 11: FAQS ABOUT STARTING A DOG BOARDING BUSINESS

- Focus on building a reputation for quality care rather than size.

How can I compete with established businesses?
  - Differentiate your services by offering unique perks, such as personalized care plans, extended hours, or eco-friendly practices.
  - Emphasize your passion and commitment to pet care in your marketing.

—-

2. Answers to Legal, Financial, and Operational Questions

What licenses or permits do I need?
  - Requirements vary by location, but common licenses include a business license, kennel permit, and liability insurance.
  - Research your local regulations to ensure compliance.

How much money do I need to start?
  - Startup costs can range from a few thousand dollars for a home-based setup to tens of thousands for a commercial facility.
  - Budget for facility rent, equipment, insurance, marketing, and staffing costs.

Do I need insurance?
  - Yes, liability insurance protects your business in case of accidents or property damage. Consider additional coverage for employees and animals under your care.

How do I handle aggressive or unvaccinated dogs?
  - Implement strict vaccination policies and require proof of vaccinations before accepting any pet.

- For aggressive dogs, establish clear guidelines and consider behavioral assessments before boarding.

What software should I use to manage my business?
- Popular options include Gingr, 123Pet Software, and Kennel Connection for booking, payment, and record management.

—-

3. Tips for Handling Difficult Situations

Dealing with Unhappy Clients:
- Listen to their concerns calmly and without interrupting.
- Apologize if appropriate and offer solutions, such as a refund, a free service, or improved communication going forward.
- Document the issue to prevent similar problems in the future.

Handling Pet Health Emergencies:
- Have a veterinarian on-call for emergencies and communicate this to pet owners during onboarding.
- Keep an emergency contact list and ensure staff are trained in pet first aid.

Managing Overbooked Schedules:
- Avoid overbooking by maintaining a clear and realistic schedule.
- During peak seasons, consider hiring temporary staff or extending hours to accommodate demand.
- If you can't take additional bookings, recommend other trusted facilities to maintain goodwill.

Addressing Employee Issues:

CHAPTER 11: FAQS ABOUT STARTING A DOG BOARDING BUSINESS

- Provide clear expectations and regular feedback to staff.
- Resolve conflicts promptly and fairly.
- Offer ongoing training to ensure everyone feels equipped to handle their responsibilities.

—-

Key Takeaways

- Addressing common concerns with a clear plan and practical solutions builds confidence in new business owners.
- Understanding legal, financial, and operational requirements ensures compliance and smooth operations.
- Proactively handling difficult situations helps maintain a positive reputation and client trust.

By preparing for these frequently asked questions, new dog boarding business owners can navigate the challenges of starting up with greater confidence and success.

CHAPTER 12: CREATING POLICIES AND CONTRACTS

Having clear policies and well-drafted contracts is essential for running a successful dog boarding business. Policies set expectations for clients and staff, while contracts protect your business legally. This chapter outlines how to establish clear terms and conditions, set policies for pet health and behavior, and draft effective customer agreements.

—-

1. Establishing Clear Terms and Conditions

Establishing clear terms and conditions is essential for any business, as it sets clear expectations for both the business and its clients. When pet care businesses provide clear terms, they help ensure that customers understand the services, pricing, policies, and responsibilities before committing. This transparency not only fosters trust but also reduces the chances of conflicts or misunderstandings down the road. For example, clearly outlining cancellation policies, payment expectations, and the scope of services can prevent confusion and ensure that both parties are on the same page from the outset.

CHAPTER 12: CREATING POLICIES AND CONTRACTS

Having well-defined terms also helps protect the business legally. It provides a framework for resolving disputes should they arise, making it easier to handle issues related to late payments, property damage, or other potential problems. A detailed contract or service agreement can outline the responsibilities of both the client and the business, which can be crucial in avoiding costly legal battles. For instance, if a pet damages property or the owner cancels services without proper notice, the terms and conditions outline how these situations will be handled.

In addition to protecting the business, clear terms and conditions also enhance customer satisfaction. When clients know exactly what to expect, including the level of care, additional fees, or specific service limitations, they are more likely to feel confident in the business. This transparency can make customers feel valued, as they understand the rules and feel they are being treated fairly. Furthermore, providing written terms gives clients a reference point to revisit if they ever have questions or concerns, ensuring clarity and consistency.

A good practice for pet care businesses is to review and update terms and conditions regularly, especially as services evolve or new regulations come into play. This helps ensure that the business stays compliant and that clients are always informed about any changes. Additionally, making the terms easily accessible—whether on the website or in person—ensures that clients can quickly refer to them and feel reassured that everything is being handled professionally.

Ultimately, clear terms and conditions are vital for maintaining smooth operations, preventing misunderstandings, and protecting both the business and its customers. By being upfront about expectations and responsibilities, businesses can foster a positive relationship with clients, leading to greater trust, loyalty, and long-term success.

Key Areas to Address:

- Booking Policies: Include requirements for deposits, cancellations, and refunds.

- Pick-Up and Drop-Off Times: Specify time windows to ensure smooth scheduling.

- Payment Terms: Outline when and how payments are accepted (e.g., upfront, installments).

- Liability Limitations: Clearly state your responsibility in case of accidents, illnesses, or property damage.

Tips for Writing Clear Terms:
- Use straightforward language to ensure all clients understand the policies.
- Make terms easily accessible on your website and in printed materials.
- Review your terms regularly and update them as your business evolves.

—-

2. Policies for Pet Health, Vaccinations, and Behavior

Strong health and behavior policies are essential for maintaining a safe and secure environment in any pet care business. These policies protect the pets in your care, your staff, and other clients by ensuring that every animal receives the appropriate care and attention, and that potential risks are minimized. When pets are well-cared for and behave appropriately, it creates a positive experience for both the animals and the people interacting with them.

One of the most critical aspects of these policies is vaccination requirements. Requiring that all pets be up-to-date on necessary vaccinations—such as rabies, distemper, parvovirus, and Bordetella—helps prevent the spread of infectious diseases. By requesting proof of vaccination from pet owners before allowing their pets into your facility, you help ensure that all animals

CHAPTER 12: CREATING POLICIES AND CONTRACTS

are protected and that the risk of disease transmission is minimized. This not only protects the health of the pets but also reassures clients that their animals will be safe in your care.

Behavioral policies are equally important in maintaining a calm and safe environment. Pets with behavioral issues, such as aggression or extreme anxiety, can create a disruptive or even dangerous atmosphere. By implementing behavior assessments before accepting pets into daycare or boarding services, pet care businesses can ensure that only animals who are well-adjusted and socialized are placed in group settings. Pets who display aggressive tendencies or anxiety may need special accommodations, such as one-on-one care or alternative boarding options, ensuring that they, other pets, and your staff remain safe.

Health policies should also address ongoing medical care, such as flea and tick prevention, managing existing health conditions, and administering medications when necessary. Clear guidelines for pets with special health needs or medical conditions ensure that staff members are equipped to provide the necessary care. Regular health checks, or requirements for recent vet visits, can also be incorporated into policies to further protect the wellbeing of animals in your care.

Ultimately, strong health, vaccination, and behavior policies help create an environment where pets can thrive, and staff can work safely and effectively. These policies set clear expectations for pet owners, establish a professional reputation, and ensure that both pets and employees are well-protected. By focusing on these key areas, pet care businesses can build trust with clients, provide high-quality care, and avoid potential liabilities.

Health Requirements:
   - Require proof of vaccinations for common diseases like rabies, distemper, and Bordetella.
   - Insist on flea and tick treatments before arrival.

- Ask for disclosure of any pre-existing medical conditions or medications.

Behavior Standards:
- Conduct assessments for new clients to evaluate temperament and suitability for group boarding.
- Create policies for handling aggressive or disruptive pets, including grounds for refusal or removal.

Emergency Procedures:
- Specify how emergencies are handled, including vet visits and associated costs.
- Obtain a signed authorization for emergency medical care.

Quarantine Policies:
- Have procedures for isolating pets that show signs of illness during their stay.

—-

3. Drafting Customer Agreements

Drafting customer agreements is a critical step in formalizing the relationship between a pet care business and its clients. These agreements serve as a written document that clearly outlines the terms of service, expectations, and responsibilities for both parties. By putting everything in writing, businesses protect themselves from potential disputes and ensure that clients understand their obligations, while also establishing trust and transparency. A well-crafted customer agreement helps avoid misunderstandings and provides a clear framework for resolving issues if they arise.

Customer agreements typically include details such as the services being

CHAPTER 12: CREATING POLICIES AND CONTRACTS

provided, pricing, payment terms, and any relevant policies, such as cancellation or late fees. For example, a pet care business might outline its pricing for grooming, boarding, or daycare, and specify any extra charges for additional services. Clear payment terms, such as due dates or deposit requirements, help clients understand their financial obligations upfront, minimizing the likelihood of late payments or disputes over costs. These agreements should also specify any necessary deposits or prepayments to secure services, ensuring that both the business and the client are committed.

In addition to financial terms, customer agreements should also include policies related to pet health, behavior, and any special instructions for the care of the pet. For instance, if the pet requires medication, special diets, or specific care instructions, the agreement can specify how these will be handled. It's also important to include clauses that protect the business, such as waivers for liability in case of accidents or emergencies, or clear expectations regarding pet behavior and the consequences of disruptive behavior. This helps protect the business from potential legal action or liability if something goes wrong during the pet's stay.

Another key element of customer agreements is addressing cancellation or no-show policies. By clearly defining the expectations around cancellations, clients are more likely to respect the agreed-upon terms, and the business can avoid revenue loss due to last-minute cancellations. Additionally, agreements should outline the process for handling any emergencies that may arise, such as medical issues with a pet or accidents during boarding. This ensures that both the client and the business are prepared for unexpected situations and know their responsibilities.

Finally, customer agreements help foster a professional, trustworthy relationship. When clients sign an agreement, they demonstrate their understanding of the terms and commitment to following the guidelines. It also provides them with a sense of security, knowing that their pet is being cared for under clear and consistent rules. By taking the time to draft comprehensive and clear customer agreements, pet care businesses can build stronger relationships with clients, avoid misunderstandings, and ensure that both parties are on the same page.

What to Include:
- Pet Information: Collect details about the pet's health, behavior, diet, and special needs.
- Owner Contact Information: Include emergency contact numbers and alternative contacts.
- Liability Waivers: State that clients agree to release you from liability in certain situations, such as illness or injury caused by pre-existing conditions.
- Payment Terms: Outline costs, due dates, and penalties for late payments.
- Cancellation Policies: Clearly explain fees or requirements for cancellations or no-shows.

Formatting Tips:
- Use clear section headings for easy reference.
- Include space for the client's signature, date, and printed name.
- Review agreements with a legal professional to ensure compliance with local regulations.

—-

Best Practices for Policies and Contracts

1. Communicate Clearly: Discuss policies with clients during initial consultations.
2. Stay Consistent: Enforce your policies uniformly to avoid confusion or disputes.
3. Be Flexible When Needed: Allow for exceptions in emergencies or unique circumstances, while maintaining overall policy integrity.

CHAPTER 12: CREATING POLICIES AND CONTRACTS

—-

Key Takeaways

- Clear policies and contracts build trust and minimize misunderstandings.
    - Health and behavior requirements protect all pets and staff.
    - Well-drafted customer agreements provide legal protection and ensure clarity for both parties.

By establishing comprehensive policies and contracts, your business will be well-prepared to handle day-to-day operations while fostering trust and confidence among your clients.

CHAPTER 13: MANAGING CUSTOMER RELATIONSHIPS

In the dog boarding business, the quality of the relationships I build with my clients plays a crucial role in the success and longevity of my business. Pet owners are entrusting me with their beloved animals, and to keep them coming back, I need to do more than just provide a safe and comfortable environment for their pets. I must offer exceptional service, foster trust, and create lasting connections. This chapter will explore the essential strategies for maintaining strong customer relationships, including how to communicate effectively, handle complaints professionally, and implement loyalty-building techniques that transform one-time clients into long-term patrons.

Effective communication is the foundation of any strong relationship, and it's especially critical in a pet care business where pet owners need to feel confident in the care their pets are receiving. In this chapter, I'll focus on the best practices for establishing clear, open lines of communication with pet owners. From the moment they inquire about services to the follow-up after their pet's stay, I'll explore how to communicate expectations, provide updates, and listen actively to ensure their needs are met. By prioritizing communication, I'll be able to reassure clients and build the trust they need to feel comfortable leaving their pets in my care.

Another essential aspect of maintaining strong customer relationships is how

CHAPTER 13: MANAGING CUSTOMER RELATIONSHIPS

I handle complaints and feedback. Even with the best intentions and efforts, problems may arise, but how I respond to them will determine whether a client stays loyal or walks away. This chapter will cover strategies for addressing complaints professionally and empathetically, turning potentially negative experiences into opportunities to strengthen my business. By handling feedback well, I can demonstrate my commitment to improvement and reassure clients that their concerns are always taken seriously.

Loyalty-building strategies are key to turning new clients into repeat customers who trust my services long term. In a competitive market, offering more than just great pet care is important. I'll explore how to offer personalized experiences, rewards programs, or special promotions to make clients feel valued. Additionally, I'll highlight how I can go beyond basic services to offer unique offerings that align with clients' needs and build a sense of community. Clients who feel personally connected and appreciated are more likely to return and recommend my services to others.

Lastly, this chapter will emphasize the importance of professionalism in every interaction. Consistency and reliability are paramount in maintaining trust with pet owners, especially since they are leaving something so precious in my hands. I'll discuss how to maintain high standards of professionalism, from punctuality and clear communication to ensuring the facility is always clean and organized. By upholding a professional standard in every aspect of my business, I'll not only gain the trust of my clients but also enhance the overall reputation of my dog boarding services.

Through this chapter, I'll offer practical tips and real-life examples for maintaining strong customer relationships in the dog boarding industry. Whether it's mastering communication, handling complaints with care, or building loyalty, these strategies will help ensure that clients return again and again—and bring their friends along with them. Strong relationships with pet owners are the key to long-term success, and by focusing on these principles, I can foster a loyal customer base and grow my business sustainably.

1. Communication Tips with Pet Owners

Effective communication with pet owners is essential for building trust and ensuring clarity between a pet care business and its clients. When communication is clear, respectful, and consistent, it helps foster positive relationships, reduces the potential for misunderstandings, and enhances the overall customer experience. Pet owners want to feel confident that their pets are receiving the best care possible, and clear communication can play a significant role in making them feel informed and involved in the process.

One of the key aspects of good communication is providing timely updates. Pet owners often worry about their pets when they are not with them, especially in a boarding or daycare setting. Regular updates—whether through text messages, emails, or phone calls—let owners know how their pets are doing and give them peace of mind. For example, a simple update about their dog's behavior, whether they are eating well, or how they interacted with other animals can reassure owners that their pets are being cared for properly. Offering the option for pet owners to contact you at any time with questions or concerns also shows that you're committed to keeping the lines of communication open.

In addition to providing updates, being proactive in addressing any potential concerns is equally important. If there are changes in a pet's behavior, health, or overall well-being, it's essential to communicate this with the pet owner as soon as possible. Being honest and transparent about any issues, no matter how small, shows professionalism and helps maintain trust. For example, if a pet refuses to eat or seems stressed, discussing this with the owner early on allows for the possibility of adjusting care routines or addressing the issue before it escalates.

CHAPTER 13: MANAGING CUSTOMER RELATIONSHIPS

Clear communication also involves setting expectations right from the start. This means explaining policies regarding vaccinations, behavior, payments, and pick-up/drop-off procedures in advance. Providing written documentation, such as contracts or welcome packets, can help ensure that pet owners understand the terms and conditions of your services. It's also important to discuss any special care instructions for each pet, such as dietary restrictions, medical needs, or preferred routines. This level of detail ensures that everyone is on the same page and helps prevent any miscommunication during the pet's stay.

Finally, listening is just as important as talking. Paying attention to the concerns and preferences of pet owners helps ensure that their needs are met and that they feel heard. This is especially true when it comes to pets with special requirements, whether it's for health reasons or behavioral preferences. By taking the time to understand the unique needs of each pet and their owner, you demonstrate that you value the relationship and are dedicated to providing the best care possible.

In summary, effective communication with pet owners is about being timely, transparent, proactive, and attentive. By offering regular updates, setting clear expectations, and actively listening to client concerns, pet care businesses can build trust, reduce misunderstandings, and foster long-lasting, positive relationships with their clients. Clear communication helps ensure that both pets and their owners are satisfied with the care provided, ultimately leading to a more successful and reliable business.

Before Boarding:
 - Provide detailed information about your services, policies, and what clients need to bring (e.g., vaccination records, favorite toys).
 - Use a pre-boarding questionnaire to understand each pet's needs, habits, and temperament.
 - Be available to answer any questions, ensuring owners feel comfortable leaving their pets in your care.

During Boarding:

- Send regular updates to pet owners, such as daily photos or messages about their pets' activities.
- Use automated systems or apps to streamline communication, ensuring timely updates.
- Be honest about any incidents, such as minor injuries or changes in behavior, and explain how they were addressed.

After Boarding:

- Provide a summary of the pet's stay, including highlights like playtime, meals, or interactions with other pets.
- Invite clients to share feedback or reviews, showing that their opinions are valued.

—-

2. Handling Complaints and Feedback

Handling complaints and feedback effectively is a crucial aspect of maintaining a strong relationship with clients and ensuring continuous improvement in a pet care business. While receiving complaints can be uncomfortable, they provide valuable insight into areas that may need attention and improvement. When addressed properly, complaints can actually strengthen client trust and demonstrate your commitment to high-quality service and customer satisfaction.

The first step in handling complaints is to listen actively. Clients need to feel heard, so taking the time to listen to their concerns without interrupting or getting defensive is essential. This approach shows empathy and understanding, helping to diffuse any initial frustration. For instance, if a pet owner is upset about their dog's behavior or an unexpected charge, letting them

CHAPTER 13: MANAGING CUSTOMER RELATIONSHIPS

fully explain the situation before responding ensures that you have all the information needed to address the issue appropriately.

Once you've listened to the complaint, it's important to acknowledge the problem and take responsibility where applicable. Even if the issue wasn't directly caused by your business, recognizing the client's frustration and expressing that you understand their concern can go a long way. For example, if there was an issue with cleanliness or a scheduling mistake, acknowledging the inconvenience it caused and apologizing sincerely shows that you value their feedback. Clients appreciate when businesses take responsibility for their mistakes, and this can often turn a negative experience into a positive one.

After acknowledging the complaint, it's crucial to offer a solution or action plan. Clients want to know that something will be done to rectify the issue. This could be offering a refund, providing a discount on future services, or ensuring that a similar problem will not happen again. For instance, if a pet was not given the proper care due to a miscommunication, offering a free grooming session or an extra day of boarding as a gesture of goodwill can show the client that you are committed to improving. A clear action plan gives clients confidence that their concerns are being taken seriously and that steps will be taken to prevent similar issues in the future.

In addition to addressing complaints as they arise, seeking regular feedback is another proactive way to improve services and prevent issues before they become problems. Encouraging clients to provide feedback, whether through surveys, comment cards, or casual conversations, helps you stay on top of client satisfaction and gives you insight into what's working well and where you can improve. Offering an open channel for feedback makes clients feel valued and shows that you are continuously striving to meet their expectations. It also demonstrates that you welcome constructive criticism and are dedicated to growing your business.

Finally, turning complaints into opportunities for improvement is key. Each complaint presents an opportunity to refine your services, whether it's improving staff training, reviewing policies, or rethinking your customer service approach. By taking each complaint seriously and using it as a learning experience, you can build a reputation for being responsive and committed to providing top-notch care. Over time, clients will trust that their concerns will be handled professionally, which strengthens the long-term relationship and boosts client loyalty.

In summary, handling complaints and feedback well is not just about resolving an issue but about building trust and improving your business. By listening, acknowledging the concern, offering solutions, and seeking ongoing feedback, pet care businesses can turn complaints into opportunities for growth and better client relationships. Clients who feel that their concerns are addressed are more likely to return and recommend your services to others, ultimately contributing to the success and longevity of your business.

Steps to Handle Complaints:
1. Listen Actively: Allow the customer to express their concerns fully without interruption.
2. Acknowledge the Issue: Show empathy and validate their feelings.
3. Investigate the Problem: Gather all necessary details to understand the situation.
4. Offer Solutions: Propose reasonable resolutions, such as refunds, discounts, or improvements to avoid recurrence.
5. Follow Up: Check in to ensure the client feels their issue has been resolved.

Encouraging Feedback:
- Use surveys or suggestion boxes to gather input on your services.
- Respond to all reviews, positive or negative, with gratitude and professionalism.

CHAPTER 13: MANAGING CUSTOMER RELATIONSHIPS

- Treat constructive criticism as an opportunity to improve.

—-

3. Building a Loyal Customer Base

Building a loyal customer base is essential for the long-term success of any pet care business. Loyal clients are more than just repeat customers—they become advocates who recommend your services to others, often through word-of-mouth or personal referrals. A strong base of loyal customers provides a stable revenue stream, allows for business growth, and can help protect your business during slower periods by ensuring a consistent clientele.

One of the key elements in fostering loyalty is providing exceptional customer service. When clients feel that their pets are in caring, competent hands, they are more likely to return and recommend your services to friends and family. Going the extra mile to personalize the experience—whether it's remembering a pet's favorite toy, offering tailored care, or simply greeting clients by name—can help build a strong, trusting relationship. Clients appreciate businesses that treat them and their pets with respect and attention to detail. This level of care makes clients feel valued, encouraging repeat visits and word-of-mouth recommendations.

Another effective way to build loyalty is through loyalty programs or incentives. Offering discounts, free services, or special promotions to returning clients rewards their commitment and encourages them to continue using your services. For example, a pet care business might offer a "frequent flyer" program where clients receive a free day of boarding after a set number of visits. These types of incentives make clients feel appreciated for their continued business, which can motivate them to keep coming back.

Additionally, having a referral program in place, where clients receive a discount or small gift for referring new customers, can expand your client base and reward loyal patrons for their support.

Consistent communication is another key factor in building customer loyalty. Keeping clients informed about updates, changes in policies, or special offers shows that you care about their experience. Regular check-ins, such as follow-up emails after a pet's stay or a thank-you card after a special event, help maintain a positive relationship. Clients who feel that they are valued and kept in the loop are more likely to stay loyal to your business. Additionally, addressing concerns quickly and professionally helps prevent dissatisfaction, reinforcing the client's decision to continue using your services.

Finally, offering exceptional care that goes beyond expectations is the best way to turn clients into loyal advocates. When clients see that their pets are receiving top-quality care—whether it's personalized grooming, special attention to a pet's unique needs, or a safe and clean environment—they are more likely to share their positive experiences with others. Providing services that go the extra mile, such as pet webcams, regular updates, or unique enrichment activities, can set your business apart and create a loyal customer base that sees the value in your offerings. A strong reputation for quality care ensures clients return time and time again, while also encouraging referrals.

In conclusion, building a loyal customer base is about creating an experience that makes clients feel valued, heard, and appreciated. By offering excellent customer service, personalized care, loyalty rewards, consistent communication, and outstanding pet care, businesses can develop a group of loyal clients who are not only likely to return but also to recommend the service to others. These loyal customers are invaluable to the growth and reputation of the business, and nurturing these relationships is key to long-term success.

Strategies for Building Loyalty:
  - Personalized Service: Remember pets' names, preferences, and special

needs to create a personal connection.

- Loyalty Programs: Offer discounts, free services, or exclusive perks for frequent clients. For example, after five stays, the sixth boarding could be free.

- Holiday and Special Event Offers: Provide discounts during peak seasons or host events like pet-friendly holiday parties to engage your community.

- Referral Incentives: Reward existing clients with discounts or free services when they refer new customers.

Engage with Your Community:
  - Host workshops on pet care or first aid to showcase your expertise.
  - Sponsor local pet events or charities to build goodwill and visibility.
  - Maintain an active social media presence, sharing stories, photos, and tips that resonate with pet owners.

—-

Key Takeaways

- Transparent and consistent communication reassures clients and builds trust.
  - Handling complaints professionally can turn negative experiences into opportunities for growth.
  - Loyalty-building strategies, such as personalized service and rewards, help create long-term client relationships.

By prioritizing excellent customer relationships, your business can cultivate trust, retain clients, and build a strong reputation in the pet care community.

Chapter 14: The Importance of Reviews and Feedback

Reviews and feedback are crucial elements in establishing trust, building credibility, and fostering continuous improvement for any business. Whether operating a small local pet care service or a larger enterprise, the way reviews are handled can significantly impact reputation and growth. Positive feedback helps to attract new clients, while constructive criticism provides valuable opportunities for refinement and development. This chapter delves into the importance of encouraging positive reviews, utilizing testimonials to draw in new clients, and managing negative feedback with professionalism, ensuring that each interaction strengthens the business and enhances its reputation.

In today's digital world, potential clients often turn to online reviews before making decisions about services. By actively encouraging positive reviews, a business can bolster its credibility and gain the trust of new customers. This chapter explores effective strategies for prompting satisfied clients to share their experiences, from creating easy-to-use review platforms to offering incentives that encourage customers to leave their feedback. Positive reviews act as endorsements, showing potential clients the level of care and service they can expect.

Testimonials, too, play a vital role in attracting new clients. When previous clients share their experiences, they provide social proof that can be more

CHAPTER 14: THE IMPORTANCE OF REVIEWS AND FEEDBACK

persuasive than any advertisement. This chapter discusses how to leverage testimonials as powerful marketing tools, showcasing authentic success stories and building a sense of trust and reliability. By strategically displaying testimonials, businesses can establish a reputation that resonates with prospective clients, helping to differentiate from competitors.

Managing negative feedback is just as important as encouraging positive reviews. In any business, there will be times when clients express dissatisfaction. The key lies in handling these complaints with professionalism and empathy. This chapter highlights best practices for responding to negative reviews, ensuring that every client feels heard and valued while demonstrating a commitment to resolve any issues. Turning negative feedback into a positive experience can strengthen relationships and showcase a business's dedication to continuous improvement.

Ultimately, the way feedback is handled can have a lasting impact on a business's reputation and success. By embracing both positive and negative feedback as tools for growth, businesses can build stronger relationships with their clients and continuously refine their services. This chapter will provide actionable tips for encouraging reviews, utilizing testimonials, and addressing complaints, ensuring that every interaction contributes to the ongoing success and credibility of the business.

—-

1. Encouraging Positive Reviews

Encouraging positive reviews is a powerful way to build your reputation and attract new clients to your pet care business. Positive reviews are more than just praise for your services—they act as a public endorsement, highlighting your commitment to quality and customer satisfaction. In today's digital age, many potential clients turn to online reviews before making decisions, and a collection of positive reviews can significantly impact their perception of your business. These reviews build trust and offer a glimpse into the experiences of others, making it easier for new clients to choose your services.

One of the most effective ways to encourage positive reviews is by consistently providing excellent service. Clients are more likely to leave a positive review if they feel that their pets received top-quality care, and if their needs and expectations were met or exceeded. A great customer experience—such as personalized care, clear communication, and friendly service—can leave a lasting impression, prompting satisfied customers to share their thoughts online. The better the experience you provide, the more likely clients will be to write glowing reviews that reflect their satisfaction.

Another way to encourage positive feedback is by directly asking clients to leave a review. After a pet's stay or service, send a follow-up message thanking the client for their business and kindly ask them to share their experience. Make the process easy by including links to review sites, such as Google, Yelp, or your business's website. Many clients are happy to leave positive reviews when asked, but they may not think to do so on their own. By making the request and providing a clear, simple way to leave a review, you increase the likelihood of receiving feedback.

Incentivizing reviews with small gestures can also be effective. Offering a discount on future services, a free add-on service, or entry into a prize drawing for those who leave reviews can encourage clients to take a few minutes to share their thoughts. However, it's important to ensure that clients are leaving honest feedback, as reviews that are seen as incentivized or forced can lack authenticity. Fostering a culture of genuine feedback will not only result in positive reviews but also build trust with future clients who can rely on real experiences.

Responding to reviews, both positive and negative, is an essential part of the review process. Acknowledging and thanking clients for positive

CHAPTER 14: THE IMPORTANCE OF REVIEWS AND FEEDBACK

feedback shows appreciation and reinforces the relationship with your clients. Additionally, addressing any negative reviews in a professional and constructive manner demonstrates that you take customer concerns seriously and are willing to make improvements. By responding thoughtfully, you show potential clients that you care about your customers and are committed to continuous improvement.

In conclusion, positive reviews are a valuable tool for growing your pet care business. By consistently providing excellent service, asking for feedback, incentivizing reviews, and responding to all reviews professionally, you can build a strong online reputation that attracts new clients and showcases your commitment to customer satisfaction. Positive reviews not only reflect the quality of your services but also help build trust and credibility, leading to long-term business success. To encourage more positive reviews:

- Deliver Exceptional Service: The foundation of any good review is a satisfied customer. Ensure your offerings meet or exceed customer expectations.
   - Ask at the Right Time: Timing is key. Request reviews when your customers are most pleased—immediately after a successful service or a product purchase.
   - Simplify the Process: Provide direct links to review platforms and clear instructions to make leaving feedback quick and easy.
   - Incentivize Feedback (Ethically): While incentives should never influence the review's content, offering discounts or rewards for submitting a review can encourage participation.
   - Follow Up: A friendly email or message post-transaction can gently remind customers to share their experiences.

Positive reviews not only improve your online visibility but also create a ripple effect, attracting more customers to your business.

—-

2. Leveraging Testimonials to Attract New Clients

Leveraging testimonials is an effective strategy for attracting new clients and building a positive reputation for your pet care business. Testimonials are powerful marketing tools because they provide real, authentic experiences from your current or past clients. When potential customers read about how your services have made a difference for others, they are more likely to trust you and feel confident in choosing your business for their pets' needs. Testimonials not only validate your services but also showcase the level of care and attention you provide.

To make the most of testimonials, it's important to collect them strategically. After a positive experience, ask satisfied clients if they would be willing to share their thoughts. A simple email or message thanking them for their business and requesting feedback can open the door for testimonial opportunities. Be sure to guide clients by asking specific questions, such as how they felt about the care their pet received or what made your business stand out. This ensures the testimonial is both relevant and detailed, offering future clients clear insight into what they can expect when they choose your services.

In addition to written testimonials, consider using video testimonials to add a personal touch. Video allows potential clients to hear directly from satisfied customers, and it gives the testimonial an authenticity and warmth that text alone may not convey. Video testimonials are particularly effective because they provide a real, face-to-face connection, helping to establish an emotional bond with your audience. A pet owner speaking about their positive experience while showing their pet enjoying your services can be incredibly persuasive for potential clients.

It's also essential to display your testimonials prominently on your website and social media platforms. A dedicated section for testimonials on your

CHAPTER 14: THE IMPORTANCE OF REVIEWS AND FEEDBACK

website makes it easy for potential clients to find real feedback from others. Sharing testimonials regularly on your social media pages can also boost visibility and reach a larger audience. For example, a testimonial paired with a photo or video of the pet in your care can be a highly effective marketing piece. The more people see positive feedback, the more likely they are to consider your business when they need pet care services.

Lastly, be mindful of the power of authentic and diverse testimonials. Potential clients want to see that your business is capable of handling different types of pets and providing a variety of services. Having testimonials from a range of clients—from those with dogs, cats, or even exotic pets—shows that you are versatile and experienced in caring for a variety of animals. Diversity in testimonials not only attracts a broader audience but also demonstrates your expertise and reliability in different aspects of pet care.

In conclusion, leveraging testimonials is a powerful way to attract new clients and build trust in your pet care business. By gathering authentic, detailed feedback from satisfied clients, showcasing those testimonials in multiple formats, and sharing them on your website and social media, you create a strong, positive presence that helps inspire confidence in potential customers. Testimonials are not just endorsements—they are a reflection of the high-quality service you provide and a vital part of growing your business. Here's how to effectively utilize them:

- Highlight Success Stories: Showcase detailed accounts of how your product or service solved a specific problem for a client.
  - Use Multiple Formats: Share testimonials in various forms, including written reviews, video clips, or even social media posts. Videos, in particular, add a personal touch and authenticity.
  - Feature Across Platforms: Place testimonials prominently on your website, social media profiles, brochures, and advertisements to maximize reach.
  - Tailor for Your Audience: Use testimonials that reflect the demographics,

needs, and preferences of your target customers.

- Keep It Updated: Regularly refresh your testimonials to feature recent and relevant client experiences.

By leveraging testimonials effectively, you not only strengthen your brand's credibility but also offer tangible proof of your value.

—-

3. Handling Negative Feedback Professionally

Negative feedback, while challenging, can serve as a valuable opportunity to demonstrate your commitment to improvement and customer satisfaction. When handled with care and professionalism, it can turn a potentially negative experience into a positive one, not just for the client but also for your business. Addressing concerns head-on and taking action to resolve issues shows clients that you are responsive, attentive, and dedicated to providing the best possible service.

The first step in addressing negative feedback is to approach it with an open mind. Rather than becoming defensive, it's important to view the feedback as constructive criticism that can help identify areas for growth. Acknowledging the client's concerns and empathizing with their experience is crucial. For example, if a pet owner was unhappy with the cleanliness of your facility, expressing understanding of their disappointment and apologizing sincerely can go a long way in diffusing tension. Clients appreciate when businesses acknowledge their feelings and take their feedback seriously.

Next, it's important to communicate the steps you are taking to resolve the issue. If a pet owner had an issue with the care their pet received, explain what you are doing to improve processes, whether it's additional staff training,

CHAPTER 14: THE IMPORTANCE OF REVIEWS AND FEEDBACK

changes in care routines, or enhancing cleanliness protocols. Demonstrating that you are actively working to prevent similar issues from happening in the future not only reassures the client but also shows your commitment to continuous improvement. This proactive approach can often turn a dissatisfied client into a loyal one who appreciates your responsiveness.

Publicly addressing negative feedback, when appropriate, can also reflect well on your business. If a complaint was made online, responding professionally and offering a solution in a public forum shows potential clients that you are proactive in managing your reputation and resolving issues. A well-crafted public response can display your transparency and your willingness to make things right, which can strengthen trust with both current and potential clients. Of course, privacy and confidentiality should always be respected, so ensure that any personal details are handled carefully and appropriately.

Finally, it's important to learn from negative feedback to prevent future problems. After addressing the immediate concern, take time to reflect on the issue and identify any underlying patterns or trends. Are there specific areas where you can improve your services? Is there a common theme in the complaints you receive? By making necessary changes based on feedback, you demonstrate to your clients that you value their input and are constantly striving to provide better care. Over time, this can help foster a culture of continual improvement and customer-centric service.

In summary, negative feedback, when addressed effectively, provides an opportunity to strengthen your reputation and showcase your dedication to customer satisfaction. By acknowledging concerns, providing transparent solutions, responding professionally, and learning from the experience, you not only resolve individual issues but also improve the overall quality of your service. This proactive approach to feedback can ultimately turn challenges into opportunities for growth, helping to build stronger relationships with clients and enhancing the long-term success of your business. Here's how to handle it:

- Respond Promptly: A quick response demonstrates that you care about customer concerns.
- Stay Calm and Professional: Avoid defensive or confrontational language. Approach the issue with empathy and a problem-solving attitude.
- Acknowledge and Apologize: Acknowledge the feedback, apologize if necessary, and express your desire to make things right.
- Investigate the Issue: Gather facts to understand the root cause of the problem before proposing a solution.
- Offer a Solution: Whether it's a refund, replacement, or additional support, offering a resolution can turn a dissatisfied customer into a loyal one.
- Learn and Adapt: Use negative feedback as a learning opportunity to identify gaps and improve processes.

When handled correctly, negative feedback can be transformed into a valuable tool for growth and customer retention.

—-

Conclusion

Reviews and feedback are more than just words—they're the voice of your customers, offering insights and opportunities. By encouraging positive reviews, leveraging testimonials, and managing negative feedback professionally, businesses can not only enhance their reputation but also foster long-term relationships and growth. Embracing feedback in all its forms is a cornerstone of success in any industry.

Chapter 15: Emergency Preparedness and Crisis Management

Emergencies are an inevitable part of any business, and the pet care industry is no exception. Whether it involves an unexpected illness or injury affecting a pet, a natural disaster threatening the safety of the facility, or a power outage disrupting normal operations, the ability to respond quickly and effectively is critical. In these high-pressure situations, preparedness and a clear crisis management plan can make all the difference in ensuring the safety of pets, staff, and the facility itself. Furthermore, maintaining trust with pet owners during emergencies is paramount, as their peace of mind and confidence in the business are essential to ongoing success. This chapter focuses on how to handle pet illnesses or injuries, prepare for natural disasters and power outages, and communicate with owners during emergencies, providing actionable strategies for managing crises with professionalism and care.

First and foremost, when pets under care become ill or injured, a swift and knowledgeable response is required to ensure their well-being. In this chapter, we'll explore how to create protocols for handling common pet health issues, from minor injuries to more serious health conditions, while ensuring all staff members are trained to react appropriately. This includes having first-aid measures in place, knowing when to involve veterinarians, and maintaining a calm, organized approach to manage the situation. Providing pet owners with timely updates during these events is also crucial to maintaining their trust, reassuring them that their pets are in capable hands.

Preparation for natural disasters and power outages is another key aspect of emergency management in the pet care industry. These events often occur with little warning, and the ability to act quickly can significantly reduce risks to both animals and staff. In this chapter, we will discuss practical steps for disaster preparedness, including emergency evacuation plans, backup power sources, and securing facilities against potential hazards. We'll also examine how to keep clients informed in such situations, ensuring that communication remains clear and efficient while emergency protocols are followed.

Clear and transparent communication with pet owners during emergencies can go a long way in maintaining their trust. When an emergency arises, pet owners may feel anxious or worried about their pets' safety. This chapter will provide guidelines for communicating effectively with clients during crises, from sending real-time updates about their pets' status to offering a clear outline of steps being taken to address the situation. It's essential to provide reassurance while being honest about any challenges, and to ensure that owners are always in the loop about their pets' well-being.

By creating a comprehensive crisis management plan that covers both pet health issues and facility-related emergencies, pet care businesses can effectively navigate challenging situations and minimize potential risks. This chapter will offer guidance on how to develop and implement these emergency protocols, ensuring that both pets and owners feel secure, cared for, and confident in the business's ability to handle unexpected situations. With proper preparation, businesses can turn potentially stressful events into opportunities to demonstrate reliability, competence, and commitment to both pet safety and client satisfaction.

—-

CHAPTER 15: EMERGENCY PREPAREDNESS AND CRISIS MANAGEMENT

1. Dealing with Pet Illness or Injuries

Dealing with pet illnesses or injuries is one of the most critical aspects of running a pet care business, as it requires a swift, knowledgeable, and compassionate response. Pet owners entrust you with the care of their beloved animals, and when something goes wrong, it's important to act quickly and effectively to ensure the pet receives the proper care. A thoughtful and well-prepared approach not only ensures the pet's well-being but also reassures the pet owner that their pet is in capable hands.

The first step in dealing with any illness or injury is to stay calm and assess the situation. It's essential to be able to quickly recognize symptoms of common ailments or injuries, such as limping, vomiting, lethargy, or abnormal behavior, and determine whether emergency care is needed. In situations where you're unsure or the pet's condition seems severe, it's crucial to have a trusted veterinarian on call, as well as clear procedures in place for emergency transport or care. Ensuring that your staff is trained to handle these types of situations calmly and effectively is essential to providing the best care possible.

Once the situation has been assessed, communicating clearly with the pet owner is vital. Pet owners often feel anxious when their pet is unwell or injured, and providing them with accurate and timely information can help ease their worries. Explain the situation calmly, let them know what actions have been taken, and outline any next steps. If the situation requires veterinary care, inform the owner of the specific symptoms to watch for and advise them on whether they should pick up their pet immediately or wait for further treatment. Being transparent and keeping the owner in the loop shows that you are in control of the situation and care about the well-being of their pet.

In addition to addressing the immediate issue, it's essential to follow up with the pet owner after the situation has been resolved. Checking in on the pet's progress or recovery shows that you are genuinely invested in their pet's health. A simple follow-up call or message asking how the pet is doing can go a long way in building trust and reinforcing your commitment to quality care. It also gives the pet owner the opportunity to voice any concerns or questions they may have about the recovery process.

Preventive measures can also play a crucial role in minimizing the risk of pet illnesses or injuries. Implementing clear health and safety protocols, such as monitoring pets for signs of illness, ensuring that all pets are up-to-date on vaccinations, and providing proper supervision during playtime, can help prevent many issues from arising. Regular staff training on first aid and emergency procedures ensures that everyone knows how to respond quickly and appropriately in case of an emergency. Additionally, educating clients on the importance of regular check-ups and preventive care can further reduce the chances of illness or injury during their pets' stay.

In conclusion, handling pet illnesses or injuries requires a combination of quick thinking, medical knowledge, and compassion. By staying calm, communicating clearly with pet owners, following up after treatment, and implementing preventive care strategies, you can ensure that both pets and their owners feel supported during challenging times. Providing this level of care helps foster trust with your clients and strengthens your reputation as a reliable and compassionate pet care provider. Here's how to manage such situations effectively:

- Recognize the Signs: Train staff to identify common symptoms of illness or injury, such as vomiting, lethargy, difficulty breathing, or visible wounds.
  - Have a First Aid Kit Ready: Equip your facility with a pet-specific first aid kit containing items like bandages, antiseptics, gloves, and emergency contact numbers.
  - Follow Established Protocols: Develop clear procedures for assessing the situation, providing immediate care, and escalating to veterinary profession-

als if needed.

- Document Everything: Maintain detailed records of the incident, including symptoms, actions taken, and communication with the pet owner.

- Keep Owners Informed: Notify the pet's owner as soon as possible, explaining the situation clearly and providing updates on their pet's condition.

Proper preparation and swift action can reduce the impact of emergencies and demonstrate your dedication to pet welfare.

—-

2. Preparing for Natural Disasters and Power Outages

Natural disasters and power outages pose unique challenges for pet care facilities, as they can disrupt normal operations and create stressful, sometimes dangerous, situations for the pets in your care. It's crucial for pet care businesses to have comprehensive preparedness plans in place to ensure the safety of both the animals and the staff during these unpredictable events. Being proactive in your preparation can mitigate risks and help maintain a sense of control in chaotic circumstances.

The first step in preparing for natural disasters is to assess the potential risks in your area. Depending on where your facility is located, you might be at risk for hurricanes, earthquakes, floods, wildfires, or severe storms. Understanding the specific threats your area faces allows you to tailor your disaster preparedness plan to address those risks. For example, if you're in a flood-prone area, elevating critical equipment and ensuring your facility has proper drainage could prevent significant damage. If you're in an area that experiences frequent power outages, investing in backup generators or establishing a relationship with emergency power providers can help maintain operations.

Staff training is another key component in disaster preparedness. All team members should know what to do in the event of an emergency, including how to evacuate pets safely, where to locate emergency supplies, and how to maintain basic care for animals during a power outage or disaster. Having designated roles for each staff member can make the process more organized and efficient. Regular drills and review sessions can help everyone stay calm and clear-headed when disaster strikes. This level of preparedness ensures that your team is ready to handle any emergency with confidence, reducing panic and confusion during high-pressure situations.

Emergency supplies are a critical part of any disaster plan. You should maintain an emergency kit that includes essentials like food and water for both pets and staff, first aid supplies, medications, leashes, crates, and any other items your facility might need to care for the animals. Stocking up on pet food, medications, and other essentials will ensure you can meet the needs of the pets in your care during a disaster, especially if regular supply chains are disrupted. Additionally, having a backup plan for how to care for pets if the facility becomes inaccessible is important. This could include temporary housing options or collaborating with nearby facilities that may not be affected by the disaster.

Another critical consideration is communication. During a natural disaster or power outage, communication with pet owners is vital. Keeping clients informed about the status of their pets and the safety measures in place can provide peace of mind. Have a clear system in place for reaching out to clients, whether it's via phone, text, or email, and make sure the information is timely and accurate. Additionally, maintaining communication with local authorities, emergency responders, and nearby pet care facilities is essential for coordinating efforts in the event of a large-scale disaster.

Finally, post-disaster recovery planning is just as important as preparation. Once the immediate threat has passed, having a plan in place to resume regular operations is crucial. This includes ensuring that any damaged

CHAPTER 15: EMERGENCY PREPAREDNESS AND CRISIS MANAGEMENT

property is repaired quickly, checking that all pets are accounted for and safe, and taking the time to review how the disaster plan worked in practice. Assessing the effectiveness of your response allows you to make adjustments and improve your disaster plan for the future. Communicating openly with your clients about how you've handled the situation can also help rebuild confidence and trust in your services.

In conclusion, preparing for natural disasters and power outages is an essential part of running a responsible and reliable pet care facility. By understanding the risks in your area, training staff, maintaining emergency supplies, and developing clear communication protocols, you can ensure that your business is ready to handle whatever challenges come your way. Preparation not only helps protect the pets in your care but also demonstrates your commitment to safety and reliability, which can strengthen your reputation and build trust with your clients. Being proactive can safeguard both pets and operations:

- Create an Emergency Plan: Develop a comprehensive plan addressing evacuation routes, safe zones, and staff roles during various emergencies.
  - Stock Emergency Supplies: Maintain essentials like food, water, medications, leashes, carriers, flashlights, and batteries.
  - Secure the Facility: Ensure windows, doors, and outdoor areas are storm-resistant and that pets cannot escape during high-stress situations.
  - Install Backup Power: Invest in generators or other backup systems to maintain critical functions, such as climate control, lighting, and refrigeration.
  - Stay Informed: Monitor local weather alerts and warnings to anticipate potential emergencies.

Periodic drills and reviews of the emergency plan can help staff respond confidently and efficiently.

—-

3. Communicating with Owners During Emergencies

Transparent and timely communication with pet owners during emergencies is crucial for maintaining trust and alleviating concerns. When a crisis arises, whether it's a natural disaster, an illness, or an injury, pet owners need to be kept informed and reassured that their pets are being well cared for. Clear communication not only helps reduce anxiety but also fosters a sense of confidence that their pets' best interests are being prioritized.

The first step in effective communication is to establish a system for quickly reaching out to pet owners when an emergency occurs. This means having up-to-date contact information for each client and being prepared to send out immediate notifications via text, email, or phone call. It's important to notify pet owners as soon as possible, explaining the situation without causing unnecessary alarm. Providing specific details about what happened, how you're handling the situation, and any steps that are being taken to ensure the pets' safety can help put owners at ease. For example, if a power outage occurs, explain that backup systems are in place and their pets are being monitored closely.

In addition to initial notifications, it's important to offer regular updates throughout the emergency. Keeping owners informed about any developments or changes in the situation helps them feel more involved and reassured. For example, if a pet's health condition worsens or the emergency situation extends for a prolonged period, timely updates on the pet's status are essential. It's also important to be honest in your communication. If there are delays, complications, or unexpected challenges, explaining them openly and offering solutions can help manage expectations and build trust.

Another critical aspect of communication is addressing any specific needs or requests that pet owners may have during an emergency. Some pet owners may want to make special arrangements for their pets, such as transferring

CHAPTER 15: EMERGENCY PREPAREDNESS AND CRISIS MANAGEMENT

them to a different location or speaking with a veterinarian. Ensuring that you're responsive to these needs, and providing options where possible, demonstrates your dedication to customer service. If a pet owner is unable to reach you directly during a busy emergency, a dedicated line or a follow-up response can help ease their worries and maintain open communication.

After the emergency has been resolved, it's just as important to communicate clearly with pet owners about their pet's well-being and any actions taken during the event. Offering a summary of the situation, including the steps taken to address the emergency, how their pet was cared for, and any follow-up care that may be necessary, shows professionalism and transparency. Additionally, providing reassurance that the situation has been handled and offering opportunities for clients to ask questions can help close the communication loop effectively.

In conclusion, communicating with pet owners during emergencies is essential for maintaining trust, reducing anxiety, and ensuring that clients feel confident in your ability to handle unexpected situations. By keeping pet owners informed with transparent, honest, and timely updates, and addressing their specific needs, you can help alleviate concerns and strengthen your relationship with them. Effective communication not only enhances client satisfaction but also reinforces your reputation as a reliable and responsible pet care provider.

- Establish Communication Channels: Use multiple platforms like phone calls, emails, text messages, or social media to reach owners quickly.
  - Provide Regular Updates: Keep owners informed about the situation, including any impact on their pets and the steps being taken to ensure their safety.
  - Reassure and Advise: Offer clear and empathetic guidance, including instructions on picking up pets if necessary or what to expect post-crisis.
  - Maintain Records: Document all communications for accountability and reference.

- Debrief After the Crisis: Once the situation is resolved, follow up with owners to explain what occurred, how it was handled, and any preventive measures being implemented for the future.

Effective communication not only ensures the safety of pets but also strengthens the bond of trust between you and the pet owners.

—-

Conclusion

Emergency preparedness and crisis management are non-negotiable aspects of responsible pet care. By addressing pet illnesses or injuries swiftly, preparing for natural disasters and power outages, and maintaining open communication with pet owners, businesses can navigate challenging situations with confidence. A well-prepared team and facility ensure the well-being of pets and reinforce your commitment to their care during even the most trying times.

Conclusion

Embarking on the journey of owning a dog boarding business is both rewarding and challenging. As you prepare to turn your passion for dogs into a thriving enterprise, there are several key takeaways, motivating insights, and words of wisdom to guide you on your path.

1. Key Takeaways for Aspiring Dog Boarding Business Owners

- **Build a Solid Foundation:** Success starts with careful planning. From creating a detailed business plan to obtaining the necessary licenses and certifications, laying a strong groundwork is essential.
- **Prioritize the Pets:** The happiness, health, and safety of the dogs in your care should always be your top priority. Trust and reputation grow from consistent, high-quality care.
- **Embrace Continuous Learning:** The pet care industry evolves rapidly. Stay updated on new trends, techniques, and tools to remain competitive and innovative.
- **Develop Strong Relationships:** Building trust with pet owners, fostering a skilled team, and connecting with local veterinarians are critical for long-term success.

2. Motivation and Encouragement for the Journey Ahead

Starting a dog boarding business is no small feat, but your dedication to caring for pets is the heart of your venture. Challenges may arise—unexpected issues with pets, operational hurdles, or slow initial growth—but perseverance, adaptability, and a genuine love for animals will see you through. Remember why you started: to provide a safe and loving environment for dogs while bringing peace of mind to their owners.

Celebrate small wins along the way, whether it's your first positive review, a fully booked weekend, or the wagging tails of satisfied guests. These moments will remind you that your efforts are making a real difference in the lives of pets and their families.

3. Final Words of Wisdom

As you move forward, keep these principles close:

- **Lead with Compassion:** Every decision you make should reflect your care and empathy for the dogs and their owners.
- **Stay Resilient:** Challenges will come, but your ability to remain calm, focused, and resourceful will define your success.
- **Trust the Process:** Growth takes time. Focus on consistent improvement rather than perfection, and success will follow.
- **Find Joy in the Journey:** Owning a dog boarding business isn't just about running a company—it's about building a life filled with meaningful connections and furry friends.

Your commitment to providing exceptional care, your willingness to learn, and your passion for dogs will set you apart in this industry. Embrace the journey with confidence and excitement, knowing that you're creating a space where dogs can thrive and owners can trust wholeheartedly.

The path ahead is full of opportunities, and with every step, you're shaping a business that reflects your passion, values, and love for animals.

www.ingramcontent.com/pod-product-compliance
Lightning Source LLC
Chambersburg PA
CBHW071026240526
45469CB00006BD/2111